The Highest Paid Employee
10 Principals of Leadership

Strategies for Regaining Focus
and
Beating Your Biggest Competitor -
Yourself.

PIA HARRIMAN

Copyright © 2015 Harriman Group, LLC

All rights reserved.

ISBN – 10: 1505862744
ISBN-13: 978-1505862744

DEDICATION

To Jason, who not only is my devoted and supportive husband, but biggest fan. You have made me a believer that everything good that is meant in your life has its own timing. Words cannot express my gratitude for the great partnership we share, especially to write this book, and to spread my message. Ryan and I are blessed to have a strong, persevering man as you are in our lives. I love you.

To Yuri, for being the P.I.A. (pain in the …) as you would say – and worked every time. For each moment you would take, patiently teaching me something about work, life and everything in between. Not everyone could understand your way of thinking, but it in turn has instilled strength and belief in their true potential once they did. I owe a great deal of appreciation to you, towards our time together.

To my sister, Mary Grace. You are the epitome of what a strong woman against adversity is. There is no excuse not to find time to write this, if I compared my hours to yours. Your story will be told through the innocent and loving eyes of your children, as well as those who have been touched by your kindness. You inspire me every, single day.

And finally, to my mother.
I never understood why you made a decision to adopt me at an older age, where most want to retire and rid themselves of any major responsibility - especially raising a new born. Yet, through this genuine act of love and sacrifice, you have literally provided a new chance at life.
With this opportunity given today, I take immense responsibility to offer a glimpse onto others of their value, as you instantly saw in me. You are my guardian angel.
I love you. I miss you.

NOTE TO READERS

This publication contains the ideas and beliefs of its author. It is intended to provide helpful and informative material on the subjects addressed. The strategies outlined in this book may not be suitable for every individual, and are not guaranteed or warranted to produce any particular results.

This book is sold with the understanding that neither the author nor the publisher is engaged in rendering legal, financial, accounting or other professional advice or services. The reader should consult a competent professional before adopting any of the suggestions in this book or drawing inferences from it.

No warranty is made with respect to the accuracy or completeness of the information or referenced contained herein, and both the authors and publisher specifically disclaim any responsibility for any liability, loss or risk, personal or otherwise, which is incurred as a consequence, directly or indirectly, of the use and application of any of the contents of this book.

Contents

Part 1:
THE "WHY" 1
WHAT DOES YOUR NAMETAG SAY 9
ALL BOSSES WERE ONCE EMPLOYEES 40

Part 2:
PEOPLE DON'T QUIT JOBS, THEY QUIT PEOPLE 43

10 Principles of Leadership

Principle #1: STAY HUMBLE 49
Principle #2: DON'T KID YOURSELF 55
Principle #3: THE PLATINUM RULE 67
Principle #4: TREAT EMPLOYEES LIKE PAID VOLUNTEERS 73
Principle #5: SHOW UP 79
Principle #6: SAY GOOD MORNING EVERY DAY .. 83
Principle #7: LEAVE A LEGACY 91
Principle #8: BE PATIENT 99
Principle #9: PEOPLE BELIEVE WHAT YOU BELIEVE 107
Principle #10: THE GRASS ISN'T GREENER ON THE OTHER SIDE. 119
ABOUT THE AUTHOR 127

INTRODUCTION

This book is centered on three cornerstones:

- **Achievement.**
  Plain and simple. I want your very core to be the essence of achievement to the next highest level. The natural progression of the human body is growth. In this book you are geared to understand how you can effectively view your life and all that surrounds it by making important decisions towards your achievement daily. You have greater abilities that lie inside you to perform at such higher dynamics you could possibly imagine. Let's discover it.

- **Professional and Personal Success Strategies.**
  The core of enhancing growth is implementing prominent strategies that require diligence and ongoing practice. You are choosing to read this book because you believe there is something greater that is meant for you – however, you must understand that it comes through work and commitment.

  This book has strategies taught by some of the most successful individuals in their own field and their own right. Use their processes and wave of thinking to create positive results in your own life and then ultimately helping others through your contribution.

- **Become a Center of Influence.**
  We need leaders in the workplace now more than ever. This book can help promote personal endeavors, but we spend the majority of our lives at our jobs and careers, so this is our focus. We need you to create a difference in other people's lives simply because they have met you, your company and your reputation. Which of these are you willing to improve or willing to jeopardize?

  "There is no one else that has the same skills, talents and experiences as you do and that is your gift to the world."

  -Pia Harriman

Part 1:
THE "WHY"

Did you ever get a chance to own your first car at age 16 or work your first job during high school? When did you get your first cell phone or computer? Were things easy to acquire from merely asking your parents, or had the ability to work for them? Imagine having neither of those options.

Growing up I didn't really pay attention to who "needed" what or what the latest obsession was out there. It only came clear during high school when all my classmates were now leaving the school premises and driving themselves out for lunch or hooky. They would buy the latest cell phone, which back then was the next best version from Zach Morris' brick on the hit show, *Saved by the Bell*. I wanted a piece of those experiences.

I got hired on my first attempt at getting a job – literally walking into the restaurant. The manager pulled me aside and asked me why I was applying today. I wanted to appease him so I said I was hoping to run and manage my own restaurant one day. He looked at me with belief and then told me to go to the corporate office to grab a uniform; I was going to start my first shift tomorrow morning.

I'm not sure if it was luck, my excitement or both. I spent the next hour with my grandfather driving to the corporate office. Did I mention it was only 20 miles away? I was so anxious, that regardless of everyone honking their horns when trying to pass us; I didn't pay any attention. I could finally start earning some real money and all to claim my own. This was short-lived.

I came to find I wasn't legal to work, as my nice, nifty social security card had a big stamp that stated, *"Not Valid for Employment"*. After all the hype of wanting to work; needing to work – I just couldn't believe it. I was quickly reminded of the manager who hired me and that he didn't follow through on what he was sending me to do. Was his role at the restaurant to play someone who signals a "thumbs up or thumbs down" for any other employee on their roster? And how could he explain his eagerness of having me start tomorrow? He didn't even ask if I was currently employed. What if I needed to put notice for quitting? None of this was stated through our six minute interview.

After two years, I was able to start employment. For a typical American, this liberty is often proved to be taken for granted. When you want something badly and finally get a chance to receive it – you make one of two decisions: you complain that it didn't happen sooner and start feeling resentment, or you graciously accept that it came through for you and proceed to enjoy it. I was thrilled at the opportunity.

In little to no time, I found myself working at a car dealership as the only female salesperson, high emphasis on female. The car sales industry already has a bad reputation; so back then wasn't any different to today. I was living and breathing these men who thought this was the easiest, get-rich-quick scenario, way before online apps. I was sent to work with a training "manager". He discussed the extremely high level of competition, so whatever it took to have the customer buy – just promise it. This meant free lifetime oil changes, or unlimited car washes at our service center and some were much worse. That by the time they drive out of the dealership, they will forget everything we would have offered them.

I couldn't do it. I couldn't lie or cheat just to get a sale. I clearly remember his words stating that if I didn't do this, I would surely fail within the first two weeks and in result being terminated. I thought this was absolutely bull crap. I put my head down, grinded away and learned everything I could about the products and the proper close ... with integrity.

I learned every make and model – horsepower to turbo engine. I learned who my competitors were and the best characteristics each vehicle provided per tier in comparison. I quickly understood why I was working so hard and doing all these things that essentially came easy for me. I tapped into my purpose. I wanted to be excellent at what I did. I wanted to earn trust in people and create an exciting experience through these vehicles and my service. I yielded over $1.3 million is sales and was the leading agent for the entire dealership - within my first 90 days employed. I guess I surpassed the two-week marker assumed.

The general manager of the dealership brought me into his office after the third consecutive month of lead sales. I've never seen an office this size. He had room for a Hummer, it was so grand. He asked why I was going to college instead of really taking the dealership on full time. Wait, really? He explained that within months I would be making six figures. He wanted to promote me to the internet sales department because back then, this was a new wave of marketing that needed my input. Was I ready to lead an entire department when I wasn't even legal to drink alcohol?

This general manager tried to promote me to help him; but didn't connect me to the idea that I could be an asset with him. You could feel the eagerness and slight desperation. I was good at my job and believed he and the rest of the management staff knew it. However, they lost sight on how this could be mutually beneficial. I could make a comfortable living while in turn providing exponential growth in revenue on their end. I could have been viewed as an asset rather than a last resort. Flattered, I declined the position and continued to work a few more weeks for the proper resignation.

No matter how you started working, why you started working or when you started working – you have a direct link on your own success. Regardless of industry, situation, environment, status, sex or abilities, it is within you to create an exceptional life; especially when it comes to your contribution to the world. I learned very quickly that businesses are successful by the right processes, beliefs and value they place on their employees and rest of the team. You have to believe in yourself, your brand and company first, before anyone else and take the responsibilities that come as being a leader.

This book is intended to help you develop your understanding of strong work ethic and the ability to shift your mind towards leadership potential. If you are in a position to oversee a team of individuals, use this book to guide yourself into creating healthy and most importantly - lasting work relationships. If you wish your own manager treated you better, differently, paid attention to your needs and those of your co-workers, then take this message and create the change of culture yourself.

We spend a third of our lifetime at earning a living; but is it only to get to the end? Many have the idea that we work towards retirement. In current insurance actuaries today, an average male, let's use men in this example – live only three years after retirement. That means, many of us are choosing to work towards dying!

There are several people work just to pay the bills, knowing that their job today, is the only way to take care of their families. These positions demand longer hours, missed birthdays, or holidays with loved ones. They cause higher stress and anxiety leading to health and relationship problems. And all for what? We weren't born to just live and pay bills.

We have the ability to create some of our first-class experiences during our day-to-day grind. Many of you will take this book as an experienced manager and go back to the basics of how you started. Use this book as a tool to create high employee retention and morale; with lessened turn-over. Use this book to guide you to formulate better strategies for your company, brand or services. This was written to help you become a true leader, no matter what position you hold.

In order to strengthen the processes in which all employees use each day; you create systems for the lifetime of the company. Become of-value to your work and see it become an asset towards your life's journey. I've had several colleagues in management roles – award winning members, who will still contact me today asking for advice on a certain individual or situation at work.

These leaders have proven themselves as strong role models to their teams, earning an immense amount of trust - and yet, they still work on this daily; as do I.

I humbly write this with the attempts of conveying a message clearly, that we need more leaders in all our industries, regarding the work place. We need to shift this mindset of having the wrong belief that the younger generation are lazy, have no ability and don't care. Becoming a leader means taking responsibility in the influence you have on others. Building teams take work. When you had your first job, we could ask your own managers how they might have thought of you and your generation as well. Would it be the same mindset you hold today?

This is not an easy fix book. We are in a society where we need instant gratification and it is ruining the capability of a remarkable experience regarding work and life. Leadership is a lifelong process and personal development is an investment. However, the rewards yield a strong, passionate character and work ethic. These in turn, results to higher staff retention, cemented client relationships and increased sales. When you earn the trust and commitment reciprocated from your employees, team and potential customers - this delayed gratification will quickly become your first priority.

I wrote this book to help guide you into becoming more consistent and how follow-through is extremely effective. However, I cannot teach you to care. Reading this book is proving to your own self the true potential that lies within you, to make a world of difference onto those who look up to you, regardless of title. Whatever your business cards state – excite yourself to the idea you can make a difference of needed change, especially at the work place.

A leader is also known as the Highest Paid Employee when he or she removes the "Boss" title and humbles themselves to the connection and understanding of their own employees. Bring it back to the basics on how you excelled and educate others around you, especially the new generation. Relating your own struggles with those same individuals you once were is a powerful message.

Leading by example is implementing you are part of the team, not just above it. This book will inspire, motivate and create daily strategies to help strengthen your relationships with those around you. After all, we are all here to live fully with purpose, not just pay our bills and die, right?

Let's begin.

WHAT DOES YOUR NAMETAG SAY?

Whether you are the president of the entire company or first time supervisor- the fact remains you weren't hired for the immense responsibility these titles hold within your first attempt towards employment. It took time; years if not decades. What if that role came unexpectedly? Were you ready for it? Before we go deeper in this topic, let me tell you the experience of how a simple change in title created a new path of awareness for me.

My first experience as a store manager was given to me at the young age of 20. Sure, there are many individuals today who are self-made millionaires before the age of eight, but this is my story.

Working at the front desk of a hotel, a district manager who oversaw the majority of Texas for his company, was so pleased by my constant memory of him every time he visited; as well as the elevated customer service, that he asked if he could offer me a great opportunity to work for him. I didn't even know what to say. I was flattered. He interviewed me and explained that he travels quite a bit, and he gets used to the same service, same routine of people he meets. From the airline attendant, cab driver and all the way to the restaurant server and front desk agents; he explained everyone seemed to blend together and the courtesies did not change hands.

However, I was different.

He stated it was my passion for how I ran my position,

with confidence and poised assertion, even though I was considered a line-level employee. It is the type of manager he needed. I didn't recognize any difference on how you were *supposed* to behave. Was the stereo-type of any hourly employee simply to run through your daily tasks and try to bypass the courtesies as quickly as possible? I'm happy I exceeded his expectations.

When he offered me the position to manage an entire loan office, I instantly stated, "Of Course!" I wasn't tied down to anyone or anything; being carefree and knowing this was a free ticket out of town. We didn't even talk about pay. I clearly enjoyed my job at the hotel. This was easily illustrated by my genuine character, which won the attention for my soon-to-be-boss. Leaving with a management title made sense. In a few months, I saw myself paying the rental fee for an 18 foot U-Haul truck and a tow hitched to my car leaving home 600 miles away. Then things started to get real.

Many of you might have entered a new role or title change unexpectedly. There is a saying that "every organization pays for training whether it has a program or not." An organization can recognize the value of training by providing a systematic approach to training delivery, thereby reaping its benefits. Or it can choose to ignore training and "pay" for training as its guests receive poor service, poor products, or poor quality, and eventually choose to go elsewhere.

There are a few companies that have not implemented yet alone, followed through with what is considered a personal development plan for their employees. A PDP plan showcases action points and steps to allow for better preparation and training onto the next step, possibly into a management role. This is also one of the common mistakes most managers fail to act upon, within their roles as leaders, by not implementing this in their company, regardless if it exists or otherwise; and taking action to build a plan or create it. This is a powerful tool towards employee retention, and if I had the opportunity to sit in on my own PDP plan at the hotel – I might have had a glimpse onto a different purpose and stayed. This proves the idea to trust the timing of things in order to make the decisions we do. We will discuss PDP plans further in the 7th principle.

When I resigned from the hotel to take on this new, and unknown opportunity several hundred miles away, the general manager called me into his office. I maybe have spoken to him three times out of the entire year, so I didn't know what this was about. He sat me down, offered me some water and asked why I was leaving. He said he had been watching me and knows that I have a great potential in the hotels and hospitality industry.

He was a gentle, older man who I looked at as a father, instantly. Yes, after only three attempts to cross paths; this was his affect. He said to give it a few years and I will be managing the front office. Wait … a few years? I had a management title already waiting for me! I quickly rushed out of his office, thanking him for his time and remember thinking *he* missed out. Was the title that powerful?

Now, let's suppose you knew your title was going to change and that promotion was nearing your way. You are probably better prepared than it coming completely unexpectedly. However, were your interpretations, physical, emotional and most importantly - maturity levels strong enough to handle these new skill sets and longer checklists of responsibilities?

To answer this question, think to yourself the number one reason you took on this new role. Was it pay? Was it entitlement? Was it because you love your boss so much, you wanted more work to ease his or her workload, on purpose? Sarcasm on that last one. If you answered yes to any of these above, the leadership role ahead is one that will take some shift in your current mindset and continued practice. Managers do not always equal leaders. It takes a solid conscious awareness of promoting growth as a whole; not just for yourself, or what your gains will be.

To showcase how titles may be skewed, I conducted this experiment:

I recently ran a poll of working class individuals from the age ranges of 18 through 56 and within several different industries. I asked them to substitute their current boss' or manager's title with a phrase that represents them. If they were their own boss, it posed quite interesting replies. I noticed a trend and of the 100 responses, I chose the top five most repeated, similar answers or phrases; whether they were negative or positive.

I'M THE BOSS, PERIOD.

Many of us have encountered this type of manager that knew it was his or her way or the highway. The lines in their management style and personality traits were so dense and the walls were 10 stories high. This is the type of individual most employees avoid. They have entered into this role as a way of passage. They were passed on from promotion after promotion during their career, or careers at different industries, when finally, it has come to their reach and will now make known to the world, they are ... the boss.

Remember my example early on? When you have wanted something so badly and it didn't arrive at your doorstep on your own timeframe or your own terms - you will make one of two decisions: embrace it or complain about it. This boss does the latter.

This commanding trait is one with little influence on maintaining a great relationship with the team. This person is often isolated and will pick and choose their *followers* with whom are made up of individuals too afraid of losing their jobs, if not agreeing to this dictator. If you are new to the employment world and this is your only boss, my condolences. Do not pick up their traits, convincing yourself that demanding and pressing are positive proofs into getting ahead in your career.

This person also feels that they are the only person that matters. Since he holds the title, it is harder for him or her to feel a sense of interdependency – the highest level of growth maturation. Basically, the ability to work as a team and embrace the different contributions that the rest of the team can uphold; thus promoting increased success. He misses out on the value of connecting with employees, and even certain key players such as potential clients and other businesses. His mindset is bull-headed.

This person also knows they are this person. You are reading this with conviction if this were you. Let me ask you – aren't you exhausted? If employees can easily state this trait or phrase representing this as you; it is not from a good place. When someone acts as they are the almighty superior, tension and turn-over rises. Employees need direction and leadership, which come from their managers and the boss. There must lie a sense of empathy and respect. Employees sense this, or lack of it.

Promotion internally has its advantages and disadvantages. One with a trait or phrase as "I'm the boss, period." more than likely came from internal recruiting; and sometimes as a last resort. Although, there are some companies that reap several benefits through internal recruiting.

Advantages of Internal Recruiting:

- Improves the morale of the promoted employee.

- Improves the morale of the staff who see opportunities for themselves.

- Provides managers with a better assessment of the abilities of internal recruits since their performance has been observed over time.

- Results in a succession of promotions for supervisory and management positions—meaning that one promotion is necessary to fill each job vacated by a promotion. These successions help reinforce the company's "internal career ladder."

- Is lower in cost than external recruiting.

- Reduces training costs since training for entry

level positions is generally less expensive than training for management positions.

Internal recruiting also has its disadvantages. If you are not careful when an opportunity of promotion presents itself you, having been originally employed within the company, the result could be devastating.

Disadvantages of Internal Recruiting

- Promotes inbreeding; after time, the flow of new ideas into the company diminishes.

- Causes morale problems among those employees who are skipped over for promotion.

- Some employees attribute promotions to friendships and relations with managers and supervisors. This may cause political overtones of being unfair and unjust.

- Creates a critical gap in one department when personnel are used to fill a gap in another.

Back in the hotel industry, there is the dreaded night audit shift. This is the graveyard shift starting at 11:00 PM through 7:00 AM. This shift is rough on most people, especially when there are very few stimuli from limited guests' presence or activity. The manager with the "boss" mindset does not comprehend that this person shows up each day, so that he, as well as other employees can sleep.

Night auditors, or those roles similarly working this shift, tend to have one of the highest turn-over rates. This stems immensely by the lack of understanding and value from those around them; especially those overseeing them. This is very prevalent to many industries. A true leader who empowers and encourages the individual taking this shift is beyond their realm of title holder.

If you manage their schedules, try and make it as consistent as possible. I honor a Monday – Friday or Tuesday – Saturday schedule, with no split days (one day working and one day off) in between. For example, if you schedule this employee to leave at the end of their shift at 7AM and the remaining hours within that *same day* is his day-off, then having him return the following night, truly does not allow this person to feel rested, or have the adequate time to visit friends or family. Having this correct balance of work and life is crucial to any lifeblood of a successful team. By hindering this balance, thinking you are being *creative* with a diverse schedule does more harm than good.

I keep this schedule in its priority throughout the year. I explain to night auditors their immense responsibility and in turn, with gratitude of covering a shift that most people won't covet, gives them a chance to enjoy quality personal time, within those two consecutive days off. Set schedules are a gold-mine for an effective team dynamic and if implemented properly; can be the baseline for high staff retention and a positive work environment.

Unfortunately, I've known quite a few night auditors who have lost friendships and relationships because this shift has created a separation in their own personal lives. When the police officer who has the late night shift leaves his wife home during the day to take care of the kids – within time can take a toll in their relationship. A leader who understands that some employees need to work to pay their bills and will sacrifice their own personal lives just to do so; will not make it harder by undervaluing this commitment and decision. Remember, you get to sleep while they work.

RELIABLE

I liked seeing a plethora of this response, in similarity to *Consistent*. Reliable managers have the ability to train others that they too, can be trustworthy and knowledgeable to the customer and clients on their own. Reliable managers are consistent with whom they help, regardless of status or title. They are also seen as Heroes when aiding a situation directly with the client; because they understand what this title holds.

Reliable is a leadership trait but in the work place, must be positioned properly. If you are an employee who may struggle on certain tasks or handling a customer complaint, a reliable manager will be a phone call or drop visit away. However, reliable does not mean tethered to the phone. Reliability has to be interchanged between the manager and its employee. You want to be able to rely on the employee after the training programs and modeling you have instilled and shown.

Reliable equals trust, credibility and empowerment. When you promise something, you follow through. When you introduce the idea that an employee has a chance to move up and get promoted, you hold true to your word and implement the empowerment onto their abilities. Many managers get into their roles and instantly start promising the world to their employees based on their completion of certain tasks, thinking this is the only way to earn this trust. Instead, this leads to conflict and disorganization within the company. It's similar to a parent promising ice cream at home if they behaved at the grocery store. Yet, when they arrive, they quickly hold back their promise because the child had toys thrown everywhere and now they have to clean that *first*; before they get their treat. This trend becomes a promise never to be fulfilled. The child ends up learning that whether they act up or continue to work; they won't have an end result. Trust is lost.

A reliable manager understands the tasks that need to be completed will be designated with follow through. For instance, if the task were to follow up on a client regarding a purchase of a home and that representative took the initiative to handle the call; the reliable manager will follow through on making sure the purchase ran smoothly, without hiccups, through all parties involved. Then naturally, it becomes expected and those employees understand the value of their actions with the reward of a consistent manager. Their presence was there throughout, even if it were to only encourage and answer any other questions that the representative wasn't aware of yet. The reliable manager directed the task and committed to the success of its result – not just handed it over; checking it off a list.

A reliable leader is also a predicable individual. The traits hold honesty and positivity. No matter if the person is the senior VP or the custodian, every interaction is done with the same amount of respect.

To become a reliable leader, you must understand that employees need guidance and follow up. Have you heard the saying, "When the cat is away, the mice will play?" There is an undertone that is placed on any manager-on-duty from their employees, with the set expectation that they will administer the rules at all times. If no one is around to enforce these rules and follow up, the company loses. Attendance (discussed in Principle #5) is key towards the success of your company. If you show up after meetings or arrive late to work, this ruins your credibility as a reliable leader. The expectation of you to lead starts hours before the employee even clocks in for the day.

BABYSITTER

For many years, there were few formal training programs for supervisors; as most development dollars were spent on hourly employees and managers at the department level or above. The hourly employees often represented the most urgent needs and the higher-level managers and executives were the ones facing increasingly complex challenges. More emphasis was placed on developing supervisors and middle managers as the quality movement revealed how important these roles were to the success of an operation.

Some companies who've adopted these training programs, did not offer true insight on why these middle managers and supervisors where being promoted from the get-go. Instead of encouraging and empowering these individuals who already had a good grasp on the company's vision, force more responsibilities with little to no communication nor proper advanced training. The result led to poor management and lack of support from a key member of the team.

The Babysitter is one who falls into this category. If they don't harbor the belief of being a valued member, they play pretend. This person watches over the team just to make sure the place doesn't burn down; but when the time is up to clock out, this person is the first one gone. Combing through the results of this survey - the babysitter had similar names such as "young", "doesn't care", "temporary replacement" to name a few. The term *babysitter* described in the poll, is someone detached from the bigger picture who often finds managing a chore.

A babysitter title does not have to be a young individual. This person does not even have to be in an hourly paid position. I've seen this style of management from owners and newly appointed managers. This individual is often short-tempered and anxious. They tend to explain to other co-workers, or worse – clients, that they are babysitting the team for the day. This showcases a demoralizing behavior towards the rest of the workers; stating, "The kids are here and need as much supervision or punishment if they act up." The title describes a manager who substitutes the command of the head of the company, taking little to no responsibility. What's worse is seeing this individual *as* the head of the company!

Now, let's suppose you entered a local restaurant and you see the employees struggling with food orders, mishandling receipts, tables that haven't been cleaned in a few hours, etc. and the owner walks up to you to say hello, as you are a regular. The first words she mentions to you are, "Yeah, it's crazy today, and the manager called in sick, so I'm stuck babysitting!" What was your instant reaction?

You probably did not sympathize with the owner. You, like most people, would take a comment like this and immediately feel there was a lack in leadership that came straight from the top! You politely take your food to-go, smile and write your low review on *Yelp*. If there is a lack of pride and appreciation from the head of the company, how can you explain or expect a different attitude from the rest? Highly motivated individuals need to be able to grow professionally. These people are often found in supervisory or middle managerial roles. If there is no value placed towards this training as modeled from its executives and higher; the company loses and the babysitters immerge.

I see it more and more how social validation and acceptance must be warranted and is highly addictive. A babysitter is unfocused at the task at hand, but craves the attention of how important they've become, per their new title. If you find yourself posting online about your nametag rather than spending time invested to the team, your leadership mastery is sitting on the sidelines. You want to play the game but have no idea how to. Validation in its own forms can be healthy and a huge motivator when needed. In essence, if you understand that you can provide your own validation without how many likes you can capture online, you can generate more energy towards the items of improvement that matter most.

A leader understands upon entering their role which involves overseeing, managing and helping a team becoming successful, to take command of the situation and proceed with action throughout every step. They also take full responsibility if there were certain instances throughout the day that caused minor setbacks; but did not allow it to stop the momentum of productivity. They do not accept the role of being a substitute, but rather the *change* needed into achieving positive results.

The leaders in place of the babysitter do not pursue traits that are skittish, agitating or impatient. They hone opposite traits that are good natured attributes; methodical and slow to react. A true leader who receives a shift in their title continues their focus on the job at hand and creates lasting processes so that the next set of leaders can easily adapt.

JUST OKAY / DOESN'T HAVE A CLUE

This title was expressed by several phrases. I received more comments than actual nametag replacements. But the collaboration of this role is someone who was promoted to a position prematurely. Sometimes this person struggles and asks the aid of others he is overseeing. This person may have been hired for this particular position as a result from not conducting a thorough interview or reference check.

A grand indicator of someone rephrased as this trait stems from the result of an external recruit. External recruiting—or hiring from outside sources—is usually easiest at the entry level, since managers can readily evaluate the skills and abilities required for such jobs. The factors that influence external recruitment strategies are all focused on the labor market, which consists of individual candidates who possess the knowledge, skills, attitudes, and abilities that meet the standards for employment within the organization. External sources also include competitors. You may end up with an individual who is not invested in your particular company, and he shows up, simply because he has the skills sets required to handle the job and knows he can get paid doing it.

Other disadvantages to external recruiting:

- It is more difficult to find a good "fit" with the company's culture and management philosophy through external recruiting.

- Morale problems can develop if current employees feel that they have no opportunity to advance in the organization.

- Job orientation for external recruits takes longer than it does for internal recruits who already know the goals of the company, how the payroll system works, and so on.

- Can lower productivity over the short run, since, in some cases, new employees cannot produce as quickly or as effectively as internal recruits.

- Political problems and personality conflicts can result when employees believe that they could do the job as well as the external recruit.

- External candidates may not prove to be as they first appear. Any external candidate is still an unknown quantity. Managers will invariably know more about an internal applicant.

Be aware how a lack in effort by not governing a

proper interview and hiring process can produce, especially towards your management roles. These lack of processes can become a major detriment in regards to the success of your business. From the responses portraying this unknown title; the truth is – employees are paying attention. This role has little to no positive influence because it is not consistent nor knowledgeable.

I went to a parochial high school. I enjoyed volleyball at its finest. I knew, however, that my skills were nowhere close to those players who attended public high school. It wasn't a lack of equipment or training – it was the schedule. The public school's volleyball team that was right next to my home, was coached by a previous coach at our own school, so I knew him quite well. I reached out to him asking if I could train with his team. He didn't even flinch. During their off-season they still were scheduled to train. In the summer months, they had a volleyball camp. I jumped at the idea of practicing with a group of people who were probably a championship or so away from playing college volleyball. It was intense.

I practiced with them religiously before my senior year. We had a new coach at our school. She was inexperienced as her coaching sessions were more about running laps around the court. You could tell that she wanted to prove herself; that she needed to. From the coaching techniques, she portrayed some familiarity with gaining wins – but, probably not at a level of winning championships.

For me, I was more than on top of my game, I was on fire! I had the best vertical of the entire team; slamming and spiking balls almost two feet off the top of the net. When it came time to evaluate the rest of the team, she saw that some girls were taller than I and some girls couldn't set the balls properly to lead the game. Because of these two factors, she placed me as permanent setter instead of the spiker. If you are not familiar with these positions, this is the position where the player sets the ball high up for the person who jumps - two feet over the net. I couldn't believe it.

This coach assumed that the different displacement due to "look" or convenience would be beneficial to the team. These decisions were far from what were really needed, or beneficial. The taller girls did not train as long as I had been previously, being I was exposed to girls almost twice my size; when practicing with the public school teammates. Their response time was much slower; thus losing a lot of games due to missed hits. What was worse was me not playing to my true potential to benefit the team. It eventually led to frustration from both coach and players, and with enough losses, tallying to her resignation.

There are quite a few individuals struggling through this transitional role. Sometimes it's a pathway towards achievement and promotion. However, there are many that pursue this role as a way through life, knowing how much they get paid and accepting little to no responsibility. Any individual venturing towards a management role with that limited mindset, not accepting the leadership responsibilities, will quickly fail due to the immense amount of obligation needed in promoting change; especially towards increasing sales and building a business.

Do you wonder if this is you? If so, first ask yourself if you are in a position of having influence towards a staff or potential clients; possibly possessing an opportunity to obtain new businesses to partner with. Picture yourself as having a team to coach. Then ask yourself if there were any productive change such as a rise in sales by a certain percentage each month, not having to fork out more payroll dollars, or the latter, having to cut costs for new-hire training? What about employee parties or incentives? Was there any room to appreciate your staff or your potential "super fans" when it came to strengthening the relationships of these promotional partners?

If you have this ability of influence and opportunity on improving the business yet, there has been little to no improvements, or you cannot afford to incent the key staff members, then you are in the *stagnation* phase. You don't create any misuse in power, or drama, or gossip but yes, your employees have labeled and assigned your title. To them, you are, "Just Okay". Is this the title you want to carry as your brand, as your leadership style? To just be okay, to be like everyone else?

In my experience, positive change such as promotions, recognition, branding, strong and loyal client relationships, etc. can all be obtained in an adequate amount of time, if you are willing to direct all your attention to it. I do not believe that you must contribute decades onto a specific role or title to gain these results. You can achieve every one of the above mentioned towards your career or company *now* – but you must be willing to put in the effort and become extremely knowledgeable.

Managers have the "Just Okay" or "Doesn't Have a Clue" title branded by their employees because they go day by day stagnantly, wishing for change, wanting change - but are not willing to put in the effort and creating it themselves. I say, *get over it!* I have no tolerance on those who take on roles of management without any desire on improvement; whether it's towards their own development and much worse – for the fulfillment of others' wellbeing while supporting your business.

When I took on the first-time manager position being a line level employee and now, onto a completely different industry, my own general manager from the hotel I was leaving did not question my ability or qualifications regarding the new role. Instead, he tried to persuade me into staying, as if I now posed an even greater asset for him. I stood out to a man that was the head of the company and had little to no direct communication towards my specific department, yet, he took the time in meeting with me and expressing the value I portrayed. My degree wasn't in hotel-management, nor possess decades of experience underneath me. I declared and exuded a strength and great understanding within my position, and that I wasn't going to play the "just okay" role. I had an unwavering belief that I was worth more than that and others believed the same thing.

By now, you can understand this is one of the worst labels as it portrays indifference and lack. The true essence of successful leadership only promotes growth from what I call – an overflowing cup. These leaders continue to work and master their own development so that it can provide value to those around them. There is no room to stop the momentum.

If you are deemed this role today, you may feel unequipped to promote leadership and change. My friend, you absolutely have this power! By understanding that a perception you play onto others can be extremely beneficial versus a lackadaisical approach, you are already one step towards achievement. If you know this, and *choose* to not take action today, then close this book now, donate it to a valuable team member, and understand that your time at your position is limited and the days towards your exceptional career path are non-existent. This is not the plan I wish for you, and everyone else who is relying on you. You have to make that decision and commitment for change today.

THE KNOW IT ALL

This person needs no introduction. You can sense them from the first point of contact and avoid them as often as possible. Why? Did you get rejected by them because your ice breaker was stating you love diet coke and they can't stand it? Then you listened to a six-minute conversation on how many ingredients are added to make it *diet* and the plethora of questions of how you could possibly like the taste of all that aspartame? These individuals can range from a first-time management role, to several decades of experience. The differentiator is that this person takes action on two things consistently:

- The decision to *not* listen and their only pauses are thinking of what to say next.

- The decision to be closed-minded or apprehensive to the ideas or support given by the rest of the team.

The truth is, this individual chooses to represent themselves in this way, as a resemblance of power, or to not be disturbed when it comes to their own personal change. In my experience, this person is an individual who is quite insecure on how to venture successfully into their roles of leadership. These are people who might have been told one too many times that their efforts or ideas were not up to par with the company; even though, those ideas could have been beneficial. They came from experiences of disappointments.

Those starting off in this entitled position of "power" have this lack of empathy towards others. It could be due to constantly having to prove themselves to their own personal relationships – parents, spouse, kids, friends, etc. that they can handle any decisions; as they can end up impacting these relationships. In result, they have been programmed that whatever they do, it is the right and *only* way.

Individuals who exude this trait of having to "know it all", are people who want to show a position of control and it comes from intimidation. I had a manager who was only a few years older than I. I state that because maybe she felt insecure of her age or that she was a woman with immense responsibilities, that possibly could've been given to someone decades older. She had a position of complete "power" being the head of the company. However, the ideas that the rest of the management crew as well as our strong connection with the staff, made it difficult to view her own value within her role. She would thank us for all our ideas, but ultimately implemented only the ones *she* would suggest, even if they weren't as beneficial towards the progression of our business.

Managers with this mindset limit their ability to admit themselves into the realm of achievement. What's worse is reprimanding their business in the process. When an individual shuts out the ideas needed to expand growth, because he or she did not come up with it first, is an extremely harmful scenario to a company. These managers do exist so how would you handle them?

These individuals aren't out for the attention or trying to constitute problematic situations within the group. It is just difficult to promote improvement when someone is not willing to listen. When you encounter this person, ask them to share their thoughts towards the ideas you presented. Then create a picture of how both would play out and agreeing to several of the positive points each plan could present.

Finally, ask them *again* how your idea could benefit the overall success of the company. By asking them to repeat this, jolts their conditioning to be aware of the situation at hand; not just to glance over and make an irrational decision because they have their beliefs that their solutions are the only way to solve a problem. You can say this is a discussion, but asking them to repeat it and following through is key towards relationship mastery.

Most importantly, be consistent with this approach. This person will start to understand that you are serious about the changes needed and it will not stop at the final result given simply because they are the boss *who knows it all.* By no means am I stating to overstep your own boundaries or respect towards your managers who act this way. This poses a different character being portrayed if this is done through malice; because you do not like or enjoy this person. The faster you understand that team collaboration works even up the ladder – you are well on your way to leadership mastery.

Let's take a moment to discuss if you do not like this type of manager. Most people state they cannot stand their "know-it-all" manager because they don't listen. If more employees or staff members took the time to break this conditioning by having a mutual understanding of processes needed through follow up questions, taking the time to link *all* the ideas presented and not settling on the one, final decision posed by this manager; promotes each parties to contribute, creating a culture of collaboration. This individual is not someone on the fence of change; but has built a habit of reacting to events hastily. Break this and you will enjoy each other's time together, harmoniously, building a successful company.

Let's review the five substitute "titles" that stood out most, regarding what employees are stating about you:

- I'm the Boss. Period
- Reliable
- Babysitter
- Just Ok – No Clue
- Know It All

What part do you play and which one do you strive for?

I do have a treat for you. Here is a bonus title:

ROLE MODEL. INSPIRATION

Again, this manager does not need introduction. This person just, *gets it*. When a situation arises, they understand their role and know the most productive ways on how to handle it – showing a great deal of mastery and dedication to their set of responsibilities.

When I mentioned he or she just gets it, comes as a result after several learning experiences and quickly utilizing it for development. It is also the aftereffect in aiding others to not experience the same pain or lessen it in regards towards their growth. They may have had their own personal role models early own and decided to take that same approach shown onto them, towards success.

Early into my own roles within the hotel industry, I made the decision I wanted to invest myself towards learning everything this industry had to offer; promoting my own personal growth; simply because I had one manager show me how enjoyable it could be.

My role model manager became proud of his own position, not even being the head of the hotel, but as the "number two". His prime responsibility was the direction of operations on the back end. He did not have authority on the final decisions towards change within the hotel, such as creating budgets, revamp in construction or demolition, etc. He did not have the direct obligation of changing the aesthetics of the hotel, which fell on the general manager or spearheading new business relationships which, a responsibility for the director of sales. Yet, he had the same respect as if he did. If he stated the remote control had to be placed in an area for easier access for the guest, yet the brand room scheme suggested otherwise – we followed suit. He stayed in his lane and perfected it.

He instilled a strong, positive influence towards the different departments and employees within. I looked at him with awe and was certain I wanted to be just like him, in his role one day. His effect towards guests was infectious and the rest of the staff loved him. We knew we would show up to an employee meeting, even if not scheduled to work – because *he* was going to host it.

Can you picture a similar influencer in your work experience, where this person made your life easier, your job more enjoyable and inspired you to contribute passionately simply because he or she was around? I told myself if I ever had his position, I would instill the same positive characteristics, as well as the environment and culture he created. He was the first to teach me that, if we have to work – why not enjoy our time together doing it.

The fastest way to increasing higher revenue, employee retention and a loyal customer base is to be a center of influence within your current role today. People believe what you believe. They will follow you for decades, and probably mention you in books they write or examples they train on, most commonly because you made a lasting impression in their lives. How powerful is this message!

A role model is defined as a person whose behavior, examples or technique geared towards success is emulated by others. To truly gain achievement, you must be able to lead by example and your contributions are impacting many more generations to come, not just the ones in front of you now.

Often times - businesses, organizations, employers and entrepreneurs lose sight on how this certain trait or title can be instrumentally beneficial towards the success of their companies. To become a successful brand – the requirement is the aid of others, even if you are a company of one. If you can positively influence these key players who affectively represents your brand, such as your employees or those loyal clients who become your biggest fans and refer you, you and your company will grow and achieve much success in speeds you ever thought possible.

Define yourself without your title. *Who are you*? There is an exercise I commence in my live training seminars where I get complete strangers to introduce themselves and not state anything personal about them. They cannot talk about their kids, what car they drive, what sports team they root for, etc. And, I allot two minutes to do so. Can you believe this is one of the hardest things people do and those two minutes seem like two hours! They get stuck! There is no conversation.

The title you have now was first decided on due to something personal in your life. A realtor in the above experiment who is limited to only express his professional status would say, "I became a realtor about three years ago. I am licensed for the state and I can show you different homes in the area if you're looking."

If you changed the way others could perceive your profession and stated this, "I give peace of mind for those who are anxiously and excited to purchase one of their biggest and most important assets within their lifetime. I help them along the process to ease them comfortably. The personal benefit when I decided to take up real estate, is for the flexibility to watch my kids' soccer games and a chance to view some spectacular homes."

Which conversation would sound more inviting to a complete stranger, who could potentially turn into a client? Which would sound remote and proving you are no different than anyone else who is in your same position or industry?

Often times we get in a position where our title represents who we are. That is far from the truth. If you picked up this book thinking you wanted to be the highest paid employee, notice that particular title doesn't physically exist in the working world. It is a perception and mindset we exude. When you get promoted or change industries, your title represents the different sets of responsibilities that change with it. The exercise above is difficult because we naturally want to talk about ourselves and to represent our values, not our daily job duties.

There should be a great sense of pride to get promoted and advance in your career; as I am definitely excited for those individuals who get to experience this change. Yet, are you now the individual who cannot be touched; cannot be spoken to unless scheduled with and all phone calls are pre-screened because you are too busy? We will discuss priorities in the 3rd principle.

Titles that are earned have the greatest advantage of truly becoming leaders than those that were easily given. Yes, promotions sometimes happen when companies need to "make more room". A promotion can be an easy fix to avoid having to hire from an outside source to fill the role - catering to a higher salary expectation, then internally where the employee may not expect much. It is the "cheaper is better" mentality; creating a sense that the term *employee* is dispensable and the people that "stuck it out over these years" can have the title with a small raise. Not every company thinks this way. The outstanding companies find ways to promote those deserving within the organization and sets aside the appropriate budget for adequate and just pay.

I take immense pride when I can promote an employee from within. I have witnessed their progression. I have seen their growth first hand. I am a firm believer in PDPs (Personal Development Plans) and their powerful impact on employee retention and quality back into the brand. Although, I too, have witnessed how their own maturity or sometimes lack of life experience get in the way of truly honing this new opportunity.

At a hotel I managed, I had the same front desk agent from the first moment of acquisition, being the hotel's new management company. He has seen the ups and downs and everything in between. He has played guinea pig on our new roll-out ideas and master IT tech on the same shift. He was a young man whose family also worked in hotels. He knew he would end up in the industry. What intrigued me most about him was his disconnection with the day to day tasks yet, with his co-workers and the guests, he was everyone's best friend and go-to guy. We knew there would be many more years shared together with him by our side. We loved every time he was scheduled. As a manager, you don't have favorites but, you know days are easier when certain people are working.

I engaged in his genuine and unique passion for life as a catalyst for his growth in the company. I encouraged every decision he made from his own intuition; in comparison to his first months at the hotel, where there was quite a bit of hand holding. I knew if I tended to this flower long enough, he would see his true potential and bloom. My hope was for him to understand that coming from a family already in the hotel industry was an indicator to fulfill his destiny.

It took one whole year for him to be promoted from front desk agent to front desk supervisor. I, unfortunately was not there when he was promoted due to being away at maternity leave. But, I knew this was his calling; and I was ever so proud.

When I returned back to work, I immediately had high expectations of him now as a supervisor. I soon realized that he wasn't ready for this new role. Did they promote him simply because he had the seniority experience? He lost his luster and his passion of service to others, which one was of his greatest assets.

He was inundated with pressures and demands because he now had his new sets of responsibilities; held accountable for being in this position. And, within a short span of a few months in the new role, he quit. I never thought he would. He loved his job, but was forced into something that didn't coincide with his current mindset or purpose and it jeopardized this. It wasn't a surprise that he took the same, original role he had and now, at a competitor company. Do not underestimate the power of comfort and fear.

COMFORT AND FEAR

When we are faced with change, especially shifting roles within our career, fear and comfort are the two top indicators to help create or prevent those impacting decisions for you. We were built to reach certain levels of feeling *safe* and avoid pain. Many people talk about the example of touching a hot stove. Once you do, you don't have to go to a different kitchen to know that placing your hand onto it, will burn.

Our brain is equipped to make changes to protect our bodies from harm. If we're not careful, we create unproductive habits and our brain turns to auto-pilot for some of the most pivotal decisions in our lives. Place this book down for a moment and look around you. Do you like the current situation you are in, within your own life right now? Don't look at your state as any worse – just look at it as it is *now*. Do you like your house? Do you like your car? Do you have a spouse or kids? Do you want any? Are you happy at your current job? Everything that you are and have today is from your conscious or unconscious decisions and how your brain responds to those previous experiences of shifting pain away.

When there is an opportunity to build or manage a company, or lead a team faced with a risk of losing a valuable employee, many react and make haste decisions, break promises and never follow through. The front desk agent in the example earlier, could have made a great career within the hotel industry, but instead chose his natural inclination to quit and avoid any more pain.

Has this happened to you? Did you try and fill the void by pressuring someone who has been with the company longer than the new-hires to lead the entire department; much worse – company? And with little to no training? This screams sunken ship altogether. Often times a company will find a need to hire from within, simply because they feel it is appropriate, and cost effective to do so; rather than taking an enthusiastic, outsider who can give a new set of eyes towards growth and success. There is no resolve when both parties – the employee and employer, share a fear of *loss*.

At this particular case, to avoid a similar situation, there are a few systems to place and steps to complete, making sure that individual is fit for the change in responsibility, and not based on seniority. PDPs, on-going training, employee recognition programs, etc. all have to be included in the core of a successful team. These systems create a trust with both the employee and the company he is representing.

Start realizing that the true understanding of an individual to go hand in hand harmoniously with your company is based on believing what you believe – first. Ideally, it wasn't for the pay. They knew what they were going to get paid at the start of hire and showed up, right? It is the value afterwards, which is placed on how they contribute back into your business that enables them to stay put.

ALL BOSSES WERE ONCE EMPLOYEES

Often times we remember only the bad repercussions when our bosses lay into our performances. I had an email sent to me from a previous employee asking for advice. She didn't know what to do when her boss took her into a department meeting and used her as an example of what *not* to do regarding the company and social media. She was quite livid.

I explained that he may have his own pressures of performance, and utilized this time to make an example for the rest of the team. Her response was an eye-opener, and often use this story when consulting managers, *"Well, that's fine, but why can't he ever remember to use me as an example when I do something right?"* She was one of the company's first employees hired and after five years, quit; entering the same role and position in a competitor company.

Employees are not against you. It takes constant and consistent effort to jab away at a specific employee to feel angst against the company; and in theory, if that is truly what's going on, then the business will fail quickly and you'll end up applying for Chapter 7.

Yes, it is easy to look at past experiences and feel that employees are only out for themselves. However, take a look back at this reasoning and those experiences that created these types of negative responses towards your belief on how an employer to employee, and vice versa, dynamic should be. When you witnessed a type of employee anarchy towards the boss, were you part of that resistance? Did you allow disgruntled employees to continue to breakdown the company, and you sat on the sidelines?

Or how about in your personal life? Have you ever encountered a waiter who has given you the worse possible service, mishandling receipts and having you wait so long for your food; ending up forgetting a few items here and there. You were surely upset, but what did you do about it? Did you take action? Did you contact the manager to help make her aware of her employee who needs more training; or did you do nothing at all and accepted it?

Some of the best leaders come out from self-awareness. These individuals know they experienced a "bad" manager, missing leadership or just a sense that things are not supposed to work this way, you know, from our good friend, that – *gut feeling*. They push for change *now*. They start to instill a positive change, no matter what position, in order to not be in that situation again.

If you are an employee wishing your manager would treat you better, offer more incentives, or praise you, you're probably right. However, you are in a more powerful position when you stop requiring this type of acceptance and take action towards your own improvement and contribution to the team. When we completely omit the idea that our own worth, especially at the workplace, is only exceptional if my boss states so, then we would be running more dynamic, successful businesses all across the board. Yes, it is hard to find the much needed energy to continue to go through the day to day *grind*, as I use that word appropriately, describing what our companies require of us at times. However, if your sole purpose is doing what you are doing right now, no other approval will feel necessary or needed.

Go back to the basics of when you were promoted yourself. How did that feel? How did this happen? Did your own managers give you the proper validation to continue? Or, did you just find a way to succeed on your own? The baseline for all successful companies is routed to the idea that growth is necessary in all forms. All forms of growth within the company is focused first on sales volume, revenue, work space, referrals and client relationships. But, where is the model for employee and staff growth?

You were once the employee who possibly wanted change and even if it didn't happen, still became successful in your own right. Are things different being that you are in this influential role now? Have your priorities changed, to what you've wanted your own manager to exhibit, towards you and the team? Or have you become the manager you once dreaded?

Things can always be different than how you once perceived the dynamic relationship of what you and your employees share. You do not have to create the same environment that might have been hostile, unproductive or political. But, you must make that decision now, in order to implement this change; wanting a better outcome for your own staff and company. You must be willing to be different. Are you in?

Part 2:

PEOPLE DON'T QUIT JOBS, THEY QUIT PEOPLE.

In this part of the book, we will discuss the 10 principals of leadership I have instilled upon myself and trained with those whom I've had the pleasure of guiding. These managers have award-winning hotels, run lucrative companies, became entrepreneurs, have strong client loyalty retention, created teams who volunteer their time away from work to help feed the homeless or visit the elderly, and show up to every meeting, every event and party - to name a few.

If you are starting off building your company and are a team of – *one*; don't fret. You will need to grow your agency, company and business by hiring a part-time individual or partnering with your accountant, marketer, etc. to help launch and continue your ramp up. This book will help you understand the crucial and fundamental starting points to do so, because you probably do not have the money to waste on dead ends and turn-over; hiring one after the other. Your influence to your partners and every potential candidate you meet is a prime factor. Understanding how to strengthen your influence can be met through these strategies. Hire now and hire properly, the first time.

In this book, you are developing yourself as a leader, who values the true importance of team building; removing themselves from the title and really honing in on the needs, strengths and weaknesses of the group. Just because you have to pay payroll from your bank account, does not give you entitlement to lose respect on potential life-long partners, who can build and support you and your business. The true makeup of a successful company is found within its people and service. You cannot simply create a product, wishing it to be a top, best-seller, just because you built it. That's being pretty naïve. It takes commitment from the people around you; those who back up the entire belief, that this is a successful product – way before everyone else does.

In this book, you will understand what creates a solid team and what allows them to break. I am a firm believer that people don't quit jobs, they quit people. I often teach this saying, "A good team is like a car. It has a specific part for a specific purpose, but alone they cannot work effectively nor complete its true purpose." Employees may quit their jobs due to relocation of the spouse, heading back to school or staying home to take care of the children, and other personal reasons. These decisions not only are drastic to the stream of income, but towards the family altogether. This is often hard for the employer to prepare for because it entails life events that occur outside work. However, the majority of reasons are due to the culture, processes and events employees experience during work.

DISASTROUS THINKING BEWARE: EMPLOYEES QUIT ANYWAY BECAUSE OF THE PAY

In 2006, a Gallup poll of one million U.S. workers had asked the question as to why they have quit a job. 89

percent of the responses were the managers, bosses, VPs, supervisors, atmosphere, you get the idea. Only 11 percent stated pay. That is a large comparison and *fear* is often the component of these results. Employers debilitate their culture due to this negative perspective that an employee will quit eventually, justifying that the pay is not enough.

Let's get real for a moment.

Yes, you create a disservice to everyone when you overload an employee without proper compensation. You see it more today how companies are experiencing higher turn-over due to simple burn out. A good employee will work hard for you if they trust in you, their company and the consistency of systems put into place, no matter who's coming in and who's moving out. However, this does not dictate the permission to abuse the good employee knowing this.

We talk a lot about paradigm shifts and resetting our brain in today's culture. It's hard enough to explain to the baby boomers and their children that businesses must rely on quicker solutions to problems, how strong their online presence is, and if you address one person – you address a thousand people, instantly. Due to our past experiences, we create a pattern in assumptions of what our future will bring. A reprimand to one disgruntled employee before, was done and over with. You do this today, and that person tells 50 other people how terrible your company is – thus, tainting your reputation.

This is the same theory of understanding how employees perceive work today. If we had previous experiences of staff leaving due to compensation; we instantly *believe* this is line of reasoning is always going to hold true. Was it truly the idea of pay? Remember, these employees knew exactly what the hourly or salary rate was upon hire, and still showed up to work. Due to some limiting beliefs, managers tend to think an employee starts performing poorly because the company can't keep up with the demands of competitive pay. It is the lack of proper training programs that degrade growth; which in turn leaves pay as one of the last indicators to retain the staff.

Price is questioned when value is missing. This is relative and holds true towards a limited belief that pay is not enough, when an employee feels undervalued. Training and empowerment builds this value and strengthens the relationships of employees towards their work.

The Walt Disney Company is a prime example of a hospitality company that takes training seriously. All new employees go through "Orient-EAR-ing," (displaying Mickey Mouse's ears) a training program lasting several days in which new employees learn the history of the company, quality standards, traditions, and even a special Disney language (employees are "cast members," who, when they are working, are "on stage," and wear uniforms called "costumes").

During training, new cast members are always reminded of the company they have chosen to work for, since reminders are everywhere. Training takes place at Disney University, classrooms have pictures of famous graduates like Mickey Mouse and Goofy, and television clips of Walt Disney himself, are shown throughout as reminders of his vision of the company and its humble beginnings. This company-wide training takes place before new recruits even step foot in their new departments. Though it may seem like overkill to the outside observer, this form of training has certainly proven successful for Disney. Annually, Disney has a turnover rate of only 15 percent, compared to the 60 percent attrition rate in the rest of the hospitality industry.

One of the most vivid examples of positive training results comes from Motorola, which spends about $150 million annually, to deliver a minimum of 40 training hours to each of its 132,000 employees (more than four percent of its payroll, far above the average one percent spent by American industries; 2010). The results are astounding. Since the program began, Motorola's annual sales have increased by 18 percent, earnings by 26 percent, and productivity by 139 percent. Altogether, Motorola employees can choose from over 600 courses offered at 14 sites; the company intends to expand its training to 80 to 100 hours per employee per year.

As we discuss into depth the 10 Principals of Leadership, note that this book should be used as a tool of reference and a management training guide. Make sure to fully read it a few more times. Leadership is an ongoing practice and takes commitment. You've made it this far to create change and success for yourself and those around you. Let's discover how to build and manifest this change together.

Principle #1
STAY HUMBLE

You're in charge, now what? Whether you came into this new role of management unexpectedly or planned – you made it. The term boss or manager does not equal leader. There is no entitlement discussed here. You must first stay humble. Stay genuine. Stay true.

When I received the call from Yuri Alvarado, regarding a position to be his director of operations (basically the "#2" for the entire hotel), I jumped at the opportunity. Yuri and I met one afternoon when I covered a front desk shift, so that he and his team can enjoy an employee party outside at the pool. As a supervisor back then, I stayed humble and didn't look down at covering a shift for a front desk agent and its responsibilities below me. To me, it felt great to take a step outside my own hotel for a change and see how other hotels operate. But this isn't my story – this is Yuri's.

He came inside the back office and we introduced ourselves. I couldn't believe the general manager of the hotel was taking the time to talk to me – *little ol' me* I would say, who was covering the front desk. Yuri is definitely unlike most people you encounter – whether manager, colleague, partner, brother, etc. He has a genuine passion all on his own, and it was exhilarating to be next to him, even just to talk about hotels. We spoke no more than 10 minutes when we soon found out we had very similar ways of thinking; especially when it comes to leading successful teams.

During this time of my life, I had a very difficult general manager. I say difficult because, in my opinion she was promoted too early to handle a great deal of stress; and worse – employees, or it seemed. Not that she didn't like people; but she definitely created that line and barrier that she was *The Boss.* That made it a very stressful atmosphere to work in. Meeting Yuri as another general manager in the same position, as you can see, was liberating.

As we spoke deeper, he asked why I wasn't the operations manager at my hotel. Again, we knew the answer to this question. My general manager felt she was capable of handling everything. It would seem I was viewed as the competition, due to a limited belief, and not ally. He quickly stated that if he ever had a chance to acquire a brand new hotel, that I would be his #2 right hand (wo)man. We laughed. What a wonderful and eye-opening experience. Almost two years had passed since we first spoke, and I received that call.

When I ended up working with Yuri at his newly acquired hotel, I was beyond ecstatic. The euphoria, anxiety and excitement arose because it was literally building a hotel from the ground up. I remember looking at the pool blue prints, and outside was only a slab of cement. Working with Yuri, I came to find he was far from just high levels of energy and borderline craziness (he will love me saying this). He knew hotels. He was extremely faithful when it came to entrusting me to manage a team and placing me as the forefront. I will be honest, I think I gave him the worst six months of his entire career; it was so painstaking. He reminds me how he would come check on me and wondered why I was staring at the computer on the same screen that had been on for the past three hours! Why I was working harder and definitely not smarter! However, he was patient and stuck with me until that flip finally switched.

When I ultimately grew into my role, I felt a whole new sense of another person emerging. Yuri never gave up on me. Every day he continued to be a pain in my ... tuckus but, never did he just push me aside. Yes, most of his teachings were to figure things out on my own; so I can learn what decisions worked best and what didn't. You must fail in order to succeed. For me, there were times I had to tell myself to stick with it; the wave of success is near. Throughout my many trials and errors, Yuri was still, ultimately the head of the hotel and took many of that responsibility (and failures) as his own; even expressing it to the owners; pressing on the idea that there is a bigger plan ahead.

Within the first 60 days being in this new role as this manager, our hotel was ranked at the barrel bottom. #235 out of 300+ of our specific branded hotels within the nation; and I can remember it clear today. Many of you in several branded and franchised industries have the same or similar ranking system. The McDonald's on 4th street is the number one in the nation while McDonald's on 12th street is #100. If you don't know about these ranking systems, I encourage you to find out.

Yuri expressed these two sentences to me when we ranked being ranked so low, "In this industry, the rank of the hotel is 100 percent the result of the leader. This is a representation of *you.*"

His message stuck with me for a while, a long while. I questioned why I was even in the industry, even as the director of operations. I thought of quitting. I was beyond distraught. Here I was, getting promotion after promotion prior to this, and then was smacked in the face with clear and concise words of wisdom.

This hit hard.

It wasn't because it was him explaining it; it was my eye-opener needed to create change. However, I had to accept it first; not making it justified by lack of team efforts, or upset guests who just write anything online, etc.; having an easy escape or excuse that any manager falls back on, even after hearing a sentence like that. I quickly shifted my mindset, reevaluated what I did on my day to day *grind*, and created checklists. I finally reached this opportunity after wanting it as a result from my ROLE MODEL manager, and I am not going to just quit.

Month after month, I trained on changing one little thing I did versus the previous day and kept working at it. I looked at each employee with a different perspective; honing on the same expectations that Yuri saw in myself. What value are they bringing and with guidance, can they be a major player in the game. It took a while to get used to hiring and firing. It was crucial and necessary to create the change needed for better service. My goal was bigger than myself. I wanted our team to represent our hotel's brand because we deserved it.

I remember it clearly when we ranked within the top 5th spot representing the brand for the entire nation. It came quick. Only six months ago my mindset was clouded by the nametag and the ego that boastfully grew, was slapped back into reality. We had surpassed over 200 hotels and in a span that some would only dream of. We were getting one great customer review after the other. The team looked at the scores *daily* as if they were going to win the lottery. It was that intense. We enjoyed every day working together. You could feel it in the air.

Naturally, a huge win like this goes straight towards the leader of the pack – the general manager. Yuri would take each accomplishment, each mention, each review, and each comment card and reverted back to me. Even though, to his own owners he accepted the responsibility, he never took credit towards the success. He stated, "Hey, I'm just here at the back – you did all the work!"

That one humbling experience made me realize how gratifying it felt, from my own manager. He was the one that pushed and guided me. He tells me to this day, I was a rare case and sometimes his way of thinking cannot always result in the same manner towards other people. I can agree to his statement, however our communication was open and honest throughout. He invested in me because he wanted my long-term growth. Ultimately, his humbleness was the powerful play here. Since then, I took the same approach towards the rest of the team I manage and oversee; and towards ongoing managers in training.

Be patient. Stay humble.

Principle #2:
DON'T KID YOURSELF

As a leader, you have to make sure every employee is positioned within their respectable and proper place, in regards to the bigger picture. Going back to my car theory – everyone plays an important part, alone they cannot work effectively. You must discern each individual strengths and weaknesses and use them harmoniously in succession with each other. Some of the best products were first formed because the inventor knew the blueprints and ingredients, then hired an accountant to manage the books and a marketing and sales rep to handle the branding and imaging; ultimately leading each other towards the same vision. To be successful in your leadership role at work, you must understand *it takes a village,* as they say. You cannot cover all the shifts, pay the bills, clean the bathrooms, run the kitchen, manage the sales and marketing, etc. You need collaboration of team members and they need their leader.

I get this question often, through the self-made entrepreneurs starting off the gate. It's hard enough having to build a business when you're left eating ramen noodles every day for lunch; then to think of the idea of using leftover funds to pay another employee. It's a hard pill to swallow. Yet, the most successful agencies who started as one broker agent, takes out a loan to pay payroll for even a part-time employee; and sees the return on his investment within the span of four to six months! The same efforts without the extra help of cold-calling, marketing, billing, etc. would take that broker agent about one to two years! That's quite a difference! Is it worth it?

You hired a part-time employee – now what? Do you have a plan for them on their first day of hire? I recently witnessed a broker agent go through the slums of hiring, even part-time help, because there was no structure throughout the entire hiring process. Upon the start of the interview, it's easy to say the positive aspects of the company, what role they would play and benefits this, that, etc. Then what happens? This agent would hire individuals who had experience in the industry, didn't have experience in the industry and sometimes just wanted a job; trying to justify that no one who is worthwhile, will work part-time. That mindset alone already paved the way of his heavy turn-over. If your goal is to have a successful company that grows throughout time; why would you only want a part-time person? They can *start* part-time; but having the right plan in place will showcase how they can earn a full-time spot by their contributions; paid through incentives and bonus programs as well. When something is *earned*, it is twice as hard to lose or give up on.

The hiring process can be exciting and nerve-wrecking for the first time manager. For the experienced individual, this process feels like a chore, is heavily overlooked, undervalued and another checklist to cross off, because there was a need to hire for a position left open. When was the last time you took part of a group or panel interview? Regardless of the position at hand, this potential candidate is representing part of the vehicle that drives your company from California to New York. Will you be successful or, will it be a vehicle that breaks down the moment it leaves the garage?

Let me take you back to the very first managing

position I held. I was to run a franchised pay-day loan store. I was now responsible for the *entire* store. That meant, profits and loss, hiring, budgets, payroll, the list continued. I had no idea what this meant. I just knew I was now getting paid a salary instead of minimum wage and the potential to have Sundays off. Yes, humor me on the thoughts of a young, inexperienced woman, but this is true to many first-time managers. It was incredible. This excitement was also short-lived.

I started noticing that we had little to no traffic of customers; but only because I assumed commercials, billboard ads or pylon signage were supposed to do that for me. Wrong. I also realized I left the busy hotel scene, with constant happy conversations of tourists bragging about the city, and how crazy their Fourth of July weekend was, to now pressing conversations of debt, signing into more debt and why you haven't paid off your debt? However, my title was "manager" so I quickly had to make the most of the situation, as I didn't want to jeopardize this opportunity, or pay grade.

My first attempt towards hiring was a bit challenging. As the store grew in its infancy months, I was told to hire more staff, starting with one. But maybe, I didn't get the memo note that morning because I thought this person was merely to cover the partial day on Saturday and we were closed Sundays. The idea to have an entire weekend off? I was beyond thrilled. Soon afterwards the mistakes kept piling, one after the other.

I was interviewing and hiring instantly. I wanted that Saturday off more than ever. My goal was to get that day covered and that was my *only* goal. Worst possible plan. I was only focused on my own needs because I brainwashed myself into believing that Saturday's sunshine was so much sweeter than any other day of the week, for some reason. I soon saw myself training just for the new-hire to "get-by" on that Saturday, handling one or two customers and perfecting a good phone script. How bad could it be – it was only a four hour shift! Little did I know, I was entrusting a complete stranger to run an entire store, and when that first Saturday "off" approached; the phone calls kept pouring in.

At the time, I felt that customer service representative I hired, never paid attention to anything I explained to her and my frustrations grew quickly. My entire Saturday morning was left tethered to the phone, as I stayed inside and stared at the clock relentlessly. I figured, she was hired for a good solid *10 days* now; this was more than enough training time! Was I so wrong. She quickly quit that following Monday and I was left only wishing for another beautiful "Saturday Sunshine".

Our attempts to cover our own wants or desires is disastrous towards what is truly needed for balance in a successful work place and team. It wasn't so much being young - I lacked control or vision of the bigger picture. I was tempted. I felt I had an invisible power to hire and put them in the exact spot I needed them to be in, for *my own gain*, and without a proper plan nor realistic and harmonious goals. I took advantage of thinking there was entitlement when at the very end, I was left by myself.

When you need to hire, first and foremost understand *why* you're hiring. Is it for the benefit of growing your company, brand or services; or is it for another gain – one that only benefits you? When you choose to mismanage your decisions, even from the paid resources given by a company, entrusted to you – the repercussion will be a huge detriment towards yourself as a leader and within your company.

In turn, interviews, when done properly are extremely valuable because this is your first vital chance to glance at individuals who can help create the business into success. Turn-over is one of the **most-expensive** cost that is hit towards a company. The majority of the time it is a result if the interview and hiring process were neglected. I then, get this response, *"People always lie during their interviews. I end up liking them and then get their evil twin at the end of the first week!"* I find this response fascinating, because many of these excuses are given, while trying to justify the lack of follow through, promised by the management team to that particular employee during the interview.

The Grand Hyatt Hotel located in downtown San Antonio, Texas has earned the Certificate of Excellence for 2014 on Trip Advisor with a four star rating. Many people, especially tourists are getting familiar with the ranking scales that Trip Advisor provides on its website. This became a powerful tool for aiding travelers on where to stay for their upcoming visit into a new city; based on previous guest reviews (go to www.tripadvisor.com for more details). A similar site such as *Yelp*, gauges reviews for retail and other local businesses.

I was fortunate to connect with a few of its lead managers and directors within this hotel and sought their framework; thus as a result to their tremendous ongoing success. They all stated the same thing, *"It starts from the very beginning, the moment they enter our building."*

For a front office position, for example, there is an interview process at the Grand Hyatt Hotel that can take up to two to three days. You have to present yourself individually to three other managers, from different departments, before reaching the front office manager. First, you must sit in on a pre-hire session regarding the history of the property; so you get to view 50 other candidates for the same or similar positions. Again, we are only talking line-level employees.

The director of food and beverage is one manager that conducts an interview with the front desk agent applying. He will want to get a sense of the new interviewee who is willing to join the team aimed at success. When witnessing this first hand that this person can handle questions efficiently; relating to room service; this then, enables him to trust they are equipped to think outside the designated department.

These leaders position themselves at the very beginning, promoting professionalism and a trust within all the departments. These leaders are not just dedicated managers, but are passionate at what they do and who they represent towards the company. They value and understand the outcome of each team member placed on property and the success it brings the business as a whole. They believe strongly in the power of interdependence.

Interdependence is the mutual agreement between two independent things that, upon relying on each other; has an enormous impact towards the rest of its environment. It is the prime essence to sustain life and grow accordingly. It exhibits the relationship and idea that we must rely on one another for strength, survival and growth.

You can understand the principle of interdependence by picturing how your human body works day to day. Your body is a vessel of muscles and cells working harmoniously and dependently together so you can breathe, think and move. They are each independent parts of the body, when removed or separated; but work most effectively together, as a whole. Working effectively and efficiently takes a conscious rapid fire from the nervous system to the brain, which then signals the rest of the body in unison. This is a perfect vehicle.

For an effective hiring process, who else will benefit from the decision of this new-hire? If you're starting off small, ask a colleague from the same company or same caliber as you, within the industry, to sit in on the interview. If you have a training employee or training supervisor, have them sit in during an interview so they know who will be entering the work place.

This attempt does one of two things:

- It provides the trainer a closer look at the new hire *as they are* before training begins. The trainer will have an in-depth understanding of your own requirements as a leader, collaborating, and towards building the strength of the team from its very beginnings.

- It shows your interviewee or potential hire how serious you value the company by showcasing your respect towards partnership and how valuable team collaboration is from the start.

When you lead by this example, you will create a trust

in one of your key, valuable players and will more than likely enhance the ongoing training process, directed by them, due from being included in the decision.

This message is also powerful all across the board, as the new hire instantly views their co-workers as a team, not separate individuals; and from the start of employment, rather than conveying an underlining precedent of who holds what title. Many times, the trainer is viewed as the person who has been in that position long enough to take on more responsibility. They have shown signs of self-reliance and a hidden passion at what they currently do.

In some instances, the trainer can be hastily assigned and its responsibilities handed on to *any* person; trying to ease on payroll dollars. Avoid this at all costs. When you assign a responsibility as training a new-hire, without proper preparation, to a senior member of the team, this is suicide towards the successful makeup of your company. Burn-out occurs from having to train and trying to keep up on their current role specific duties; because a promotion or adequate training was never implemented.

By properly executing ongoing training; as if you were having these individuals take over the entire company one day; should be the mindset of any leader. Start your focus that everyone will become this valuable member and you will have an infectious environment, having everyone wanting to learn from each other. We will discuss further in **Principle #7 – Train for Your Replacement**.

Make sure you properly incent this "trainer" employee with a pay increase if you are formally or informally placing them in this role; as you're having new hires work beside them. Remember, you are removing them from their day to day comfort zones; but, as an already, well-oiled part of the vehicle, and now shaking them and giving them a whole new set of responsibilities. Don't fear this change. This is healthy if done correctly. Let me show you:

Appoint one to two employees for this role so that the expectation of training will be consistent. This will *not* hurt your bottom line. Incentives and small pay increases are highly effective and extremely beneficial because you are investing a small monetary exchange, but in turn, will produce a huge profitable outcome; freeing your precious time for other corners of growth that can use your focus. This also enables retention from these key employees, feeling trust in you as their leader and continued growth. This reduces turn-over and varied labor costs.

Our habits, experiences and perception change the muscle memory of our bodies, as previously explained, over the course of our lifetime. A person who smokes daily, for example, may experience certain cells having to work harder to maintain this organic system. However, over time, too much of those overworked cells will die and parts of the body will be critically if not permanently impaired. By paying close attention to the high signals in your brain screaming, "Stop abusing us. We need help. We are dying ..." will take a conscious effort to change the situation before it's too late. This is the same effect regarding the bloodline of your business and success within your team. Too much poison will affect the entire vessel.

Just like our body, if we find our teams in stagnation, eventually they will no longer work. People need constant stimuli to aid in their sense of purpose. In turn, this provides better results toward productivity, increased retention and can be extremely lucrative overall.

THAT ONE EMPLOYEE

Talk about weeding out the poisonous crop. An employee with a constant bad attitude is worse than setting half the building on fire. I say this with conviction. This employee sucks the life out of everyone else they surround; thus rippling the effect onto the customer, team, and the list goes on. Nowadays, the repercussion is negative, having online social media reviews about your company, which can be devastating towards your brand.

This particular individual can be shifty and sneaky towards management. You may not notice which ones these are at first glance; but pay attention to the culture when they're on the clock. I've had my share of overseeing these types of people, but more often do I witness this employee in other businesses - when I'm the *customer*. It's much worse!

I often visit small, local businesses for the majority of essentials and necessities when I can. I absolutely love local Texas coffee. I have a designated local beauty salon and local restaurants I visit on a frequent basis. This is a norm for many Americans. We like what we like and we make it a daily habit. My ultimate favorite is utilizing these small businesses to aid other businesses. Referrals are the best way to grow your business.

Upon visiting a local coffee shop for over a few years now; I've become one of their "regulars". I enjoy and reap the rewards of having my same drink already being whipped up the moment I stand in line. Local coffee places attract the "newbies", so their typical order time can run from 5-7 minutes; which is taxing to a regular. I also get much acquainted to the baristas and staff; but there is an ongoing theme in this particular shop – so many new employee faces to keep up with!

For the ones that *"stuck it through"*, in their words, have opened up an array of frustration from their day to day grind. But, I feel I have a good indicator on those genuine frustrations, which come for broken systems and that one employee - who likes to stir the pot. Usually, this happens to many organizations; and often it's too late to detect the cause because so much damage has ensued. They waste other people's time and roll their eyes in front of other customers, after receiving a reprimand; thinking this is ok. And this person, from the moment the owner walks in, will showcase the biggest smile; exuding the warmest welcome. "Fake, fake. Fake. Fake." – Elaine, *Seinfeld*

I witness it happening in front of me so many times, at several different businesses, that I want to pull these owners aside and let them know they have a problem in their hands. However, this is often the result of rushed interviews and applicants to fill bodies on the spot – not honing in on *why* they are hiring to begin with. What's worse is having some owners know that this is going on and with a defensive attitude; will accept it, due to cutting costs from new-hire training, or is too overwhelmed with the rest of the business to put forth much needed effort.

If you are fully ready to create change and lower turn-over, in result towards high retention; even in a small coffee shop, gas station, retail shop, just to name a few, you must first look at how you view your employees and the way they view you. **Don't kid yourself.** These employees can easily jump ship at the next local coffee shop down the street; but has cleaner bathrooms, even though they are the ones to clean them, because the training program instills follow-through, greater value to that staff member and a positive, working environment. Remember, its only 11 percent of individuals that quit due to pay.

Get rid of the bad seed. You will eventually find this person quickly and no, they are not your best friend or best hire. They come to work late with a multitude of excuses and will act busy to throw off your attention during the first hour; having you "understand" they did not mean to keep you and your employees waiting. They waste your time; complaining about everything. If they can easily vent to you about their problems and the problems of other employees at work; they do not respect your time as their manager nor your goals as a business owner.

If this person has one true strength that is detrimental to their role; give them a 30 day coaching and counseling notice. By giving them a chance to be part of the team, rather than against it, even after you have witnessed these compulsive tendencies; will show true ownership on their part and leadership on yours. It is a binding promise from the both of you to make this relationship a healthy one. Once the plan is in place and acted upon; you will soon experience a different set of employees; different attitude towards clients; and a different culture revealed.

Principle #3:
THE PLATINUM RULE

Many of you heard the Golden Rule – *"Treat others the way you want to be treated."* We have all been nurtured to abide and live by this rule for peace and harmony; especially at the work place. The premise of the Golden Rule is believing everyone thinks, acts and feels the same way *you* do; and that they should. There are several variations to this rule, but the most impacting I have experienced and still abide by today, is the Platinum Rule: "Treat others as how *they* would want to be treated."

This message is a powerful one, as it takes true listening and understanding of the other individual; especially those seeking out your assistance. It removes the proposition that our needs are the priority over theirs; jeopardizing a strong connection and service.

On one of the hotels I recently acquired to manage, a guest came down to the front desk; flustered, because he thought a housekeeper had stolen his newly purchased cologne. At first, he brought it up to one of my team members stating that he must have misplaced it; but instantly, the agent tried to give peace of mind, and explained to the guest that we will certainly ask our staff to help find it as well.

A few days pass by, and the guest asked for any news. Still nothing. A little over a week goes by and he stops by the desk and still no sight of his cologne. Note, we have several guests who visit for work in the oil fields, so they tend to stay months at a time. That particular moment, the executive housekeeper was walking down past the front desk. She noticed the gentleman and his flustered look as he was veering back to his room. She asked him how his day was going. He explained, "I'm fine, but I can't find my cologne. I know you have a great staff, because I've ended up asking every single person here and believe them that they haven't seen it. They've been nice to check up on me about it. I possibly left it in my bag and it may have fallen out hauling my stuff from different company truck to different truck. But, I figured I would try to ask the team again."

At this moment, she quickly asked him about the cologne, wondering why it was so important. "It was my father's favorite cologne and loved it growing up. He just recently got sick, so I figured I would get it for him to remind him of him wearing it while we were around; so it would spark a good memory. We shared a lot of good memories together and I would remember his smell thinking of them. But, it's extremely expensive, so I don't have the means to pay for another one; that's why I keep checking that maybe someone turned it in at the front desk."

Instantly, she asked for the name and where he can find it. It was no more than $65 but still a hefty price tag; especially for this young worker. She asked him if he was able to buy the cologne again and if so, we will reimburse him. She came directly over to me, explaining the *on-the-spot* decision she had made; and if we couldn't reimburse him as a hotel – she would pay out of her own pocket. Not knowing if he truly lost it or a temporary employee in the housekeeping department might have taken it, she knew it was the right thing to do. I said, "Absolutely! Let's take care of him." He left that evening and came back with the receipt. His impression was beyond shocked and appreciative. The staff stood there, smiling.

I am still proud of that team today, as it takes a moment to stop and listen to someone's request. During the infancy of forming this great team, an example of leadership was shown on how to treat someone the way they would want to be treated. Not everyone has the ability to offer to pay for a replacement; and that was far from my expectations of them. However, the executive housekeeper knew, as her desire to lead a successful team and brand of service; she did the right thing.

I instantly used this example on the next employee meeting and asked how each person would have handled this situation differently the next time. Answers from across the board flared. Every single staff member, regardless of department was able to provide an adequate answer. They all agreed they should've sought better clarity from his situation sooner. You cannot leave a decision made like this, by another employee or staff member unnoticed. You must celebrate it, showcase it and have it become a platform of training the other team members of what to do next time. This harbors trust as the team acknowledges as a whole - the true instinct based on the decision to provide service; not just promising free stuff to guests who complain.

Then after finding out the reasoning that this was his sick dad's present; many offered to pay for it as a collection between the team. Some offered to call the dad's room in the hospital and send him some flowers, pictures of the staff or visit. Because the real reasoning why this guest wondered about his cologne, was that it reminded him of great memories shared together; in hopes that he would feel happy during their difficult time now.

Everyone had the ability to contribute to this guest in his or her own form. The team understands that they must assist the situation based on listening to the guest; then providing a resolution on how the guest could ultimately benefit. They are not limited to the four-walls that confine them, when clocking in. Personally, if a hotel staff did these above ideas mentioned regarding the last time I misplaced my work-out shoes – I wouldn't expect them to pay for it! The Platinum Rule breaks the bounds of assumptions, by focusing on that next level of leadership.

As a great leader, we find ourselves treating others the way *they* would want to be treated. We do this from example. If we only treat our counterparts, department heads, supervisors, and bosses with respect– we harbor the precedent that only "title" matters. If we treat our employees with the same adoration and understanding we do for our guests and clients; the shift in culture will manifest.

If you are acquiring a new ownership or inheriting a team, the first step towards this change is hosting an employee meeting. I remember a hotel we took over, had the same employees working together for several years. They never celebrated each other's efforts, birthdays, accomplishments or understood why they were all doing what they do. Instead, their belief was simply to feed their families and work. The first month of taking over, all I thought about was when we were going to host the next employee meeting/celebration. Why? Employee meetings and celebrations are a great tool for strengthening team collaboration and harvesting a healthy and enjoyable work environment.

During this meeting; start your approach about *them*. Explain where the company's goals lie and are geared towards. Explain how this particular team, group, department, etc. can help be its catalyst or vessel towards achievement, enhancing scores, increases revenue, branding, the list continues. This should be an all-engaging affair. Employee meetings shouldn't last more than an hour to an hour and a half. This is also a planned process. For your supervisors and department heads; or for those individual agents and entrepreneurs – your key decision team members' meetings should be face to face on nearly a weekly or daily basis. No pressing information should be pushed off later, as in waiting for the employee monthly meeting to start.

My employee meetings/celebrations weren't just pizza and prizes and talks about rates or pricing. I had several team collaboration and building exercises that focused on each team member; having them explain how they couldn't do their jobs without the help of the other employees. This not only built rapport but most importantly – a conversation. Employees were willing to share ideas on how to build a better brand. We had a ton of laughs. Some employee meetings ended sooner than planned because the staff was so eager to get back to work and try-out what they already had learned within the first 15 minutes! Try implementing this to the monthly routine and training for the staff. Employees want to feel valued and just as important, want to feel included.

Yes, it is understandable that you can get busy. When an employee expresses a concern in their own job duties, take the time to answer them by scheduling a meeting within the next 48-72 hours. If you end up directing them to wait until the next employee meeting, which might end up having them wait for the next 20 days - can be damaging to their perception of you. You are showcasing this employee is less important than your current tasks. Remember, they are part of your company's success if you allow this to happen and take the necessary time to aid in their growth or concerns; before they talk to a competitor employer about it.

Depending on the nature of the concern; analyze if you are the best person to answer or assign it to another fellow manager. Just do not wait and put off an employee's needs. It may be hard for some employees to bring any concerns to their managers, so this is a major opportunity to connect back with the specifics of the team. They have the expectation you are busy; but scheduling time to address their own concerns pose a perception exceeding this expectation and deposits pieces of trust and admiration into your pocket as a respected leader. Treat them how *they* want to be treated and start to see and feel the culture shift from good to great.

Principle #4:
TREAT EMPLOYEES LIKE PAID VOLUNTEERS

Dare I say it? Yes, this creates an irony of the previous principals and what you've learned throughout this book regarding a shift in your mindset; omitting the belief that employees have a short shelf life; and are willing to leave sooner than later. So why am I state to treat these employees like paid volunteers? Just like a volunteer, they are *not* part of the team; they just invest their time and move on, right? Quite the contrary.

Ok, Pia, how the heck am I supposed to do this? Well, it's quite simple. Why do volunteers, volunteer? First, they understand there is a need and they can fill that need. Employees like to contribute, because, well, they're humans. Some of the greatest philosophers affirm this, as well as the oldest forms of discovery state, there is one common distinction between humans and the rest of the planet: *The good that is birthed within a man's heart is his ability to contribute.*

A true volunteer gets involved in whatever they do simply because they *want* to do it. They invest their free time into it. They do not expect to get paid for it. They understand that there is a need for their labor to help a greater good. They wake up early for it and don't come home until the wee hours of the night because that's what it has asked for. They say it's a labor of love and we need more of these patriots.

Now, take what a true volunteer represents and envision this towards all your employees. If you start to believe that you have individuals willing to wake up early to come in and provide their own labor of love in what they do towards work; the pay ends up being a bonus. You treat them as if they are irreplaceable and a valuable piece of the picture; emerging your energy with synergy toward their passion to work. A great deal of genuine appreciation is amplified through your actions because of this belief. You start noticing and believing that they care about you and the business.

No matter what the job entails, people like to help other people. It is your responsibility to create an atmosphere of service and contribution. Quality service does not go straight to the customer that is willing to spend an extra $1,000 on their tab in hopes for a better tip. Service is given freely from the heart; to help aid a person's life or experience and make it better.

This goes without doubt at the moment of hire. Explaining the description of what the job entails, is one form to commence a good hiring process. Without hesitation, connecting how this person's strengths can help enrich the role they are entering, creates importance; and confirms that their own abilities are truly desired, versus simply hiring another body.

We hire to complete what was missing *as a whole,* in replacement of the critical part – not a substitution. When you hire a body, you set the tone for the other employees that they are *disposable*.

Back in the 1950's bakers would start work extremely

early in the morning, preparing the dough, so when it was sold - you could literally imagine it being baked just seconds before you arrived. It was fresh. Nowadays, there are machines that remove these delicate hands so that bread can be mass produced. You lose the sense of freshness.

If you take some of the best, upscale restaurants in upper Manhattan, New York today. The *Modern – Dining Room* located on 9 West 53rd Street is a great example. The bread alone was literally baked that same morning. As much profit as they generate; they do not believe in purchasing a heavy machine to alter and replace this delicate process. The chefs take pride on committing to their bread – which is just the filler that is served before the actual, prized main courses. This was no accident.

These chefs, just like the 1950's baker took pride in their diligent process and the results of their products. This takes loyalty. This takes passion. A good leader focuses on the strength of its employees and truly enhances their passion at the love of working. They do not hire machines or bodies just because they can *do* the job. You take a bigger chance in standing out, going above the competition, when you don't do things exactly the way everyone else does; only to mass produce yourself.

How does this look like when you are hiring a volunteer? Just like having an assembly line to feed the homeless; everyone has a position. Make sure you have a clear outline for each role. When I start my interview process, I commit to having my training manager and two other department heads with me. They each are well prepared and are assigned on which questions to ask, while I make the final explanations of expectations. This allows my training managers and supervisors to get better experienced at their interviewing skills with my guidance. Also, I am there to aid trust yet, verifying that the process is properly executed. Do not overstep your other hiring managers when they are performing during this time. This is *not* your role.

Being interdependent on each other's attempts to hire and given perspectives, will enhance the hiring exposure as well. Remember, these staff members sitting in with you are on *your* team. When they feel this inclusion, trust continues to form and the hiring process will be a crucial, yet enjoyable part. In addition, I set up the final interview with a sister-property manager or similar manager in my role on a different date, asking the questions without me present.

If you have a small team, a training manager/shift leader present is fine to start. Then, follow through on that second interview. Interviews are more frequently rushed than ever and as result having underdeveloped employees. The second interview gives you another perspective if this person is consistent in nature, as well as you having another day to gain perspective. This interview process has to be pre-planned; noting that a good, solid hire will be developed within the next 60-90 days, not four.

Collect your evaluations from each interviewing member and collaborate. Introduce your thoughts on certain prime subjects that pertain to each role. Every interview must always include how they can enhance the productivity of the person they are working with. What a concept! When employees gain a better perspective in their roles of providing service and contribution through your products, true-buy in is established. They find themselves with a different mindset and setting their own personal expectations; which can lead to appreciation and value on their day to day endeavors.

Rid yourself of the negative thoughts and assumptions of what may happen. Realize you have today, as a new start for the success of your company. Remove the doubt that employees will leave you and start treating them as paid volunteers. There is a type of appreciation felt throughout the team, when this is the perception led by you. You create respect. You understand that their efforts are contributed solely because they wanted to – from the start of applying to work *with* you. The pay is their bonus because they *want* to be there. Celebrate this.

Principle #5:
SHOW UP

Early in my career of managing a mid to high level hotel, and overseeing several departments, I understood there was an expectation of me to enforce the policies of tardiness and absenteeism. It was hard for me to comprehend how people couldn't show up on time, even if it meant costing their stream of income, as termination was the result of several *no-show,* lack of attendance. Yet, when it came to attending employee parties and events; everyone was exceptionally present.

Regardless of the day to day, a good leader shows up, no matter what. What this means goes beyond just attendance. This means commitment towards your character, professionalism and brand. This consistency is portrayed as a leader and you are willing to be part of the team. Managers who gradually walk in during the peak hours or 15 minutes late for a team meeting are deemed as lazy or cannot comprehend the ability to evaluate time, in my opinion. You portray a displacement of entitlement, thinking it is ok to just show up, because another manager is hosting the meeting. There is little to no forgiveness here. Title has no play. What is worse is trying to befriend a few employees to forgive your acts of tardiness, thus blurring the lines of employee / employer expectations altogether. Respect is lost.

When we are consistent with our actions, we are reliable. Sometimes, we fall into our own realm of processes and performance as managers, and lose sight of the bigger picture. I was guilty of this, when I journeyed towards the "accountant's" mindset. Sometimes, it took all day, having to sit behind my computer to figure out payroll, invoices and PDP's. I became *comfortable* for having only one or two conversations that were outside my technical devices, emails or texts. I quickly learned that leaders aren't leaders if they don't have anyone to lead. My computer didn't follow me. If anything, I followed it. I knew my presence was beyond captivating and important, and I was nowhere to be found if I was sitting behind my computer screen.

This goes with your promises, not just towards your staff – but to your vendors, your clients and own families. Do not commit towards an appointment you cannot keep. There are several individuals who are handicapped with fear of leading a team, dreading having the face to face conversations or sales presentations; and it's only getting worse as our technology makes communication easier to hide behind these devices. Some individuals have another team member host the trainings, meetings, or client presentations and will tag along for "support". You are physically present but not committed – so you showed up, just to – show up, not paying attention to the conversations of landing key business partners; and this is *not* what I'm talking about in this principle. This does nothing for you or your professional growth.

Fear is what can motivate you or paralyze you. Fear stops you from showing up on time, making you seem unreliable. Fear stops you from learning about other employees and what drives them, in result to help them grow within the company, from a fear that getting too personal might allow them to use it against you. Don't get me wrong, you should never make a team member feel uncomfortable from asking what their activities were off work, the night before. But, it is healthy to understand where their values lie, and can be a huge contributor of motivation; helping them understand that working together is beneficial for both parties. Fear is assuming all answers are no, all people are the same and this is just how it is. Fear is limiting. Fear is defensive. Fear allows businesses to shut their doors for good.

I have consulted quite a number of companies and small businesses to help them reignite their own fire and message towards success. When I would meet some of the owners, their first impression resulted in lost hope, fear and all in all in a burnt out state. I remember thinking, I was a heavily, sugar-dosed cheerleader, trying to tell them the - *"You can do it!"* mantra, when they had little to no energy to express the same. But, when action took foot, they were engaging back into the business, into their staff and *showing up* both physically and mentally in all aspects that were needed. They remembered the prime reason they started their business and found this new wave of energy.

I've had managers tell me they only work at certain times of the day; and are only "supposed" to come in and out during this time, and blah blah ... Wait? Who's running the company? There are several managers who feel this entitlement; so they justify their work hours and times they are "supposed" to show up. How has this become beneficial towards the team? Many times, there are owners who have their managers cover certain shifts as the line-leveled employees, to try and save on payroll cost. In turn, the direction of who is in charge is faded; because there is physically, no one in charge.

When you show up, you must show up early and show

up every time. You will definitely need the help of many other individuals who can take care of issues that you're not as passionate about; and this is ok. For employee engagement, we commence our monthly employee parties. I can rely on the executive housekeeper and supervisor to plan the cake, food and decorations. I personally, do not hone these skills; especially to the caliber and excitement they do. They in turn, feel part of the overall picture and we celebrate this together.

If you created the brand, then hire an accountant for the budgets and numbers. If you're not as personable face to face, make sure the one individual representing you at the front end has the best attitude, presence and knowledge to take on this role. Then you show up consistently behind the scenes, rewarding their efforts through incentives, appreciation, simple thank you cards, employee of the month recognition and so much more. When you show up consistently after your team's efforts of service and contribution, which is in-line with your company's vision and success goals; you are creating sustainable retention and life-long trust.

Also by showing up, you get to experience all the benefits that your company goes through, like meeting a profitable business partner, who also likes to golf on Saturday mornings. Or the opportunity to launch the new renovation scheme and take a sneak peak on the color palettes. These are small, yet great examples of what you can appreciate when you are consistently present. You will be remembered often as well. It is the affect you have on your team and if you truly hone in on the importance of building your positive influence with those around you, doing this is a start and the result of that influence is quite powerful.

Principle #6:
SAY GOOD MORNING EVERY DAY,
NO MATTER WHAT

Basically, this principle means respect. Respect anyone and everyone you encounter. Respect is not a trait you're born with. Respect is an action you contribute to your fellow man. There have been sayings that respect is earned, not given freely. In my opinion, I disagree to this mantra. I firmly believe that when you give respect freely *first,* you earn it wholeheartedly. This doesn't mean, however, that I'm an inexperienced, business professional. If trust and respect are lost – they will be extremely difficult to regain back, if at all.

I say good morning to every single face I encounter once I land on property. Each individual deserves my attention, even towards physically being there. Why? Because the guests and clients who showed up before I, experienced their warm smiles and service. The grounds are kept clean. The bathrooms are stocked. Each member of the team plays a vital role, so why is it justifiable to only give respect to those that have the greater titles, responsibilities or corner offices?

We are inundated with so many emails, messages, texts that it can pose someone to go on auto-pilot when responding. I make a conscious effort to start each message with, *"Dear Someone, hope you had a wonderful weekend. How was the golf tournament ... "* I learned this from a few managers before me, which clearly stood out beyond the crowd. The president of this company would always start with a short message, asking how my son is doing, or husband and then went about the content of the business within the email. Then, I would have another manager who didn't even site my name, just went on one to two sentence rants on getting this or that done. I could feel how valued, or *not* I was, through an email opening. It was a powerful message.

Character is *not* what you do. Character to me, is defined by *your ability to see the purpose birthed inside you and to live by no other standard than your best.* I could've easily gotten upset at the manager in my previous example, who asked me to do A, B, and C but couldn't even recite or acknowledge my name. However, I'm better than this and work for a higher purpose. I understand how much on auto-pilot some executives can be, but too much on auto-pilot will devastate the morale of the workplace and successful makeup of the company.

Needless to say, your chances of building a prominent team dynamic are extremely heightened by placing respect *first*. It does not show weakness – rather the opposite. I have been asked this several times, in more ways than one, how managers who do not want to show weakness, think it is okay to assert command in everything they do; wondering why their turn-over is so great. The result of the president's actions were favorable, due to these little gestures of respect; and filtered down.

This almost always, shows how humans create a relationships with their job and what they do. They want to feel valued, but most importantly respected. You, as the leader - have the prime responsibility of creating a successful business and gilding strength in your team. By displaying respect, in retrospect, is by acknowledging your team working at all hours; having you and the other key players, rest or focus on the other major improvements towards building the business, for example.

Ultimate respect comes from relieving that individual to tend to a family crisis or personal situation, because family is the primary importance to any working individual. They can say they are 100 percent dedicated to their job, but if they don't have anyone to share their earnings with, or to validate their commitment back at home, they will soon burn out and will be a complete detriment towards your business.

Lesson: When an individual says they have no one at home, this is false. Make sure to ask who is most important in their lives and what makes them so. Create these connections and respect their relationships early on to make sure you are gaining the same respect back towards your company.

Billionaire entrepreneur and investor – Marcus Lemonis, from CNBC's hit prime show, *The Profit,* goes to struggling businesses and helps bring their companies back into working and lucrative order. He sometimes does a complete re-branding of the original name of the company itself. In essence, he is there to invest and make money.

Lemonis has a straight-forward approach towards building successful businesses. However, he does point out, from time to time, that the best employees hired are those who do *not* have families at home. I am conveying this segment here, because even as a billionaire investor, you don't have to think this way to heed successful change. It is a collaboration of respect and trust given to each valued team member that creates this success. Yes, it is *easier* to handle employee schedule changes; when someone is not relying on that member at home. By creating a sense of value, stemming from each member – within each role they play; will not matter if they have a spouse, child, step-brother or family pet waiting for them at home; that will jeopardize their contribution at work. When appreciation is missing, the blame come pouring in.

Respect does not mean favoritism. As a strong leader – your ability to work with everyone will set you apart from the rest of struggling businesses. Many managers often find themselves favoring one employee or staff member, more than another, especially in that other person's presence. They will forgive tardiness because this person is likable. They often speak highly of this person more often than others.

To sight individuals, who are achieving greater success, more rapidly, than other employees as examples, are a good way to help guide the team towards heightened expectations. However, make sure your words don't create an invisible bubble, that this person who is improving, is untouchable. Respect comes towards the understanding that each staff member holds merit. By connecting their own relationship and perspective, as to how your business can truly be a great experience for each employee; will create a buy-back into your company. Employees like to see role models; but also want to feel that same respect and excitement in their own good deeds.

When you engage and allow each member to participate in the assessment of team collaboration, services and even branding; you are exhibiting a great sign of respect. Issuing *Informal Participatory Techniques* work well in most operations to gain employee feedback and buy-in. Remember, your focus is the lifelong commitment of your company's succession and its growth within.

Informal Participatory Techniques:

In most operations it is relatively simple for a concerned and interested supervisor to use informal methods to gain employee participation. Consider, for example, the situation that arises when a decision must be made, perhaps about a recurring problem that must be resolved. You might begin by writing the ways to resolve the problem you can think of, then follow this up with a request for other ideas from affected employees. In doing this, you could talk to:

- Every employee affected by the problem

- Informal group leaders

- Experienced employees only

- Selected employees whom you think would have specific ideas or would have special interest in solving the problem

Talking with any or all of the above employees will likely generate helpful alternatives. As you continue with the problem-solving task, participating employees could be involved in determining:

- Advantages and disadvantages of each alternative

- Procedures for implementing the selected solution

- Methods for evaluating the effectiveness of the solution

- Ways in which the solution may affect other aspects of the department

As you consider whether to involve employees in decision-making, be aware that disagreements can result—and that the disagreements must be managed. You will need to address conflicting interests and may need additional time for decision-making. Also, it's sometimes difficult for even the best-intentioned employees to remain objective; their own personal biases and concerns can influence their participation.

When you decide to involve employees in problem-solving and decision-making activities, it's important that the task at hand really involves employee participation and not just persuasion on your part. In final, respect is an exchange and should be mutual.

There is an expectation towards each specific role to complete its tasks. Just because you say hi to the valet attendant every morning; doesn't give him permission or a sense of entitlement to act up or take cars off premises, and not clocking out for lunch, for example. These are examples of theft and insubordination, which results in termination.

Respect is the true mutual understanding that I'm

placing value and faith onto you for helping me build my business to achievement.

Principle #7:
LEAVE A LEGACY
TRAIN FOR YOUR OWN REPLACEMENT

You are just getting the hang of leading a successful team and now, you're training for your move out? Quite the contrary. When you enter a realm towards a new title, a new responsibility or role, one of your main responsibilities as a leader, is making sure there is someone there to replace you. You are not placing the precedent that you are quitting. You are cementing the idea that you are continuing to grow and are committed towards the legacy of the company to lie in the same, good hands of the next generation.

There are several findings and theories about evolution that really fascinate me. One basic understanding of our human cells is its need and ability to grow. In just one week, your entire body will shed its old skin cells and reproduced new ones. You are an entirely different person 52 times throughout the year.

Our brain is just the same. Our basic survival needs can be summed by having water, food, shelter, oxygen and sleep. There are several others but these are the five basics. In quantum physics and neurosciences, we are starting to understand, or being re-introduced to the theory that our body, including our mind, needs to grow to be just as effective as having the five basic needs for survival. For example, we tend to create goals in the beginning of every year. Why do we do this? Is it a trend? Then, by Jan. 15th about 92 percent of Americans fail to attain their goals. In essence though, was it to truly create change or just a list of things you *don't* want in life? I don't want to smoke. I don't want to have bratty children. I don't want to eat donuts every morning.

The 8 percent of those who achieve their goals end up going back to their old patterns because they don't know what the next step is. Create a new goal! People state that they want to work hard enough to retire. Actual insurance studies state that a typical man, (let's use American Men in this example) will die only three years after retiring! So, to work towards retirement means to work towards death!

Truly, to try and only work to reach an end is not the right aspect or wave of thinking any strong leader would take on. When you have reached the ability to create change in your own professional environment; then take the responsibility of teaching this to the next generation. This way you are far from just wanting to die. You are creating value and purpose within your life. You are in constant action and fulfillment and thus, your legacy.

Remember that feeling you had when you opened your first set of business cards? If you haven't it's quite a memorable experience. It didn't even matter the title, just the mere fact you had a card to state your "importance" towards the company. I've seen cards with just the direct number to the business yet, the person who had their name on it was gleaming ear to ear when she handed it out to me.

When you take on the responsibility of creating value for a person taking your place, you have another loyal piece of the puzzle. The brain, for example, is nurtured by learning from new experiences. When you promote professional development and growth, with consistent follow-up; generating a precedent that there is potential for advancement, you will omit the stagnant employee trolling online through Instagram, looking at different work out tips or desserts, placing someone on hold for 15 minutes.

As a true leader, if you create value in any employee, you teach yourself how to discern quickly who can benefit from replacing your role and who still needs time to improve. Don't let this deter you in thinking that you need to terminate the ones not making the cut. Remember, a good team is like a well, oiled car. All parts are necessary to function. Yes, even the radio antennae.

You learn to practice what your company is looking for to succeed as well. Your business plans will grow as desires, accessibility and the market assessments of your customers' needs expand as well. You gain control of situations arising through these changes, because you learn what your players have to offer.

The biggest piece of advice in advancement is always know how to play the game. When I mean the game – I mean the goal, life, and career – whatever needs achievement. We are placed on this earth with purpose. You cannot leave your company without knowing the next step is to continue your own professional or personal growth goals. Then there is no purpose in life for you and this is a sad truth. You have gone this far, reading this book, and I'm sure having other forms of trainings and motivation, to help you achieve your lifetime goals that will continue to fuel your purpose as well. If you don't know what your purpose in this world is now, I'm telling you, there is one. Of the 5.5 billion residents on this earth, if not more - have our own unique purpose placed here. There is not one other person that has the same skills, experiences and talents you have. That is your gift to the world; and your purpose.

By teaching and instilling what we have learned from our previous experiences, making it easier for the next generation to follow suit, is a great indicator of a strong leader. In the workplace, most managers, unfortunately, have a fear of being replaced, so they shy away from training what they know onto others; thinking those staff members need to *just figure it out*.

Unfortunately, I have met my share of these individuals. They experience so much lack in their life and the real truth behind some of their own internal promotions, have been due to cutting labor costs, or from a hasty, last minute decision. They were never nurtured or guided into their own value and to understand the importance they play towards the company, already as they are. They feel this is their only way to showcase their worth to the world; so they will protect someone else from stepping in and taking it. If you firmly believe that this is your only set of worth, hopefully by now you come to realize, you have so much potential and capabilities towards achieving success.

I wanted the director of operations position more than any other role imaginable in hotels. Yes, even becoming a general manager and CHA (The **Certified Hotel Administrator** (CHA®) Online Review is a certification honored by the American Hotel and Lodging Education Institute) hotelier, which is higher than the director of operations. It was the role in my hospitality career I truly coveted. I had a great role model who played this role and an unfortunate perception towards the current general manager at the same time, so you could understand what enticed my curiosity, when it came to setting up my goals towards advancement. When I finally achieved the director of operations position, I was in for a whirlwind.

Going back to the time when Yuri was teaching me anything and everything on how to run the hotel through his general manager's point of view, I first started to question his master plan. Wait ... that's not my job! I thought I was here to learn how to operate the hotel as the director of operations? It took several months to understand that he had this unwavering faith in me to soon take over my own property as a general manager and when that role comes to fruition, I will easily mend into it. He was absolutely right. When you excel and climb higher in your rankings, positions or roles within your company; there is little to no hand-holding. The expectation is there to make sure you are fully equipped and prepared to run the company efficiently and effectively.

I learned he did this greater service to me because in a few months, I was handling and understanding budgets that usually takes a few years to master. I know several employees who sought to advance and yet no one took the time to sit down and plan the exchange of knowledge. Again, this stems from their own fear, territorial fear. When you understand that creating a set of leaders following you will not only validate your true character; you omit these blockers towards your growth. You owe this to yourself. Professional development and continued adult education should always be pursued, regardless of advancement in title or services. It promotes growth needed to live a more fulfilled life; especially at the workplace.

Take this self-less act of dedication towards developing the new generation; seeing that employees are *not* the competition, but in fact your biggest ally. You will perceive a greater sense of reward towards your company; as well as your own role as leader.

Start implementing and delegating certain tasks to those around you, that can be beneficial towards their maturation and understanding of what they do. The key to these successes are follow through. Remember they do not have your role, *yet* – so they may not fully grasp the bigger picture until it is practiced often. Also, they are learning; so if you continue to just pour loads of your own responsibilities and justify this as "training", will eventually lead to burn-out; in result, losing one of your biggest and best employees and supporters.

Helping supervisors become better at their jobs can have a dynamic effect throughout the organization. As supervisors receive training, they are likely to become more effective in the way they manage people. In turn, the people they manage may become more productive and contribute more to the organization. The effectiveness of training and development for managers will largely be measured by the success of the organization or the department that they manage.

Depending on the organization, different variables will be used to measure success. For example, some organizations will measure only profitability. Other companies will measure numerous factors such as: employee turnover, repeat customers, rates and pricing, food and beverage costs, waste reports, productivity per hour, on the job accidents, etc. There are several assessments that help create a lasting legacy on your behalf.

When you find yourself teaching others, you also become an expert in your craft. Many individuals who retire find themselves writing or blogging about what they have learned throughout their course of their careers. They create workshop classes in different industries. This too, can be a great concept to understand, knowing that retirement does not equal loneliness or boredom.

You also, don't have to retire to share your knowledge. Being an inspiration to like-minded individuals in your field today, will inspire others to know similar goals are attainable, especially in this work climate; as they mirror your same procedures.

When you train for your own replacement, you are offering value within yourself. Let's use an NBA basketball team, for example. Taking over as coach of the San Antonio, Spurs in 1996, Greg Popovich is the longest tenured active coach in both the NBA and all US major sports leagues. He is one of only five coaches in NBA history to win five or more NBA championships. He has definitely gone through his roster of different players; but his lessons, coaching and style never falters, year after year.

Popovich doesn't short change any player. Some may criticize him as playing safe or fair, by trying to have every player hit their feet on court during each game. But his leadership is what stands clear. He understands that every player has the ability to help the team win; not just individually – but as a whole. And he has been consistent throughout each generation. Yes, many of these players will replace him one day, if not coach their own leagues and be the Spurs' competitors, but the value is precedence through his forever actions, in his day to day responsibilities as a leader.

Principle #8:
BE PATIENT
HOW DO YOU EAT AN ELEPHANT?
ONE BITE AT A TIME

Upon reading this in today's society, you know we have a slight addiction that craves *instant gratification*. Where did this all start? We discovered that when we post a picture online of our cat or our favorite lasagna recipe and other people "liked" it; we became addicted for this type of validation.

Nowadays, when everything revolves around being convenient, products are sold by the troves on how to make the average individual even more lackadaisical towards work and efficiency. People want their needs and goals to be fulfilled now. It is why my previous example on goal setting, takes an average of 15 days for the majority of the nation to try and take needed action for change; but, due to prolonged or delayed results, end up quitting. Goals take time to achieve; they take patience.

This goes towards any successful business goal, team building, brand rankings, increased sales, client retention, and true leadership mastery. To achieve heightened success, it takes a process, especially all 10 principles to be repeated weekly if not daily. Successful leaders are creatures of positive habits. They instill the correct motivation, push and reflection towards their staff with little to no effort, because it has been fully engrained within them. Tapping into your true contribution and purpose has to rely on the understanding of patience. You cannot change the world overnight; but you must have the unwavering faith that it will change – effectively and appropriately to fill your purpose.

If someone emails or texts me about how they're currently dealing with a difficult staff member; I can instantly go on a rant on helping this person flip their perspective back to their own values. I shift their focus on their systems and if they're engaging, empowering and developing their employees in the realm of the success of the company. It is what I do, what I live for. I am passionate towards others finding their own fire within themselves because that same respect was given to me. It may not affect them, in that moment, but it will. It takes time.

You can be an expert in your field and want the whole world to validate how brilliant you are, whether it's online, through emails or emoticons. This habit has little to no value back towards your growth, both physically and emotionally, and you do not learn in the process. When you dedicate yourself to professional development or higher learning; which fosters a relationship on an idea you do know, and something you discover; puts you on the right path towards success mastery. When you pave the way for others to follow suit on this type of mastery, you now become a brand, a trademark, a net worth of true potential. These pathways are also streams of time. Systems and follow through are most efficient when proper time passes; allowing the brain and body to create positive reinforcements and take action. These turn into habits; thus birthing character.

For example, you have given your sales manager a project to provide for you three natural markets that contain your targeted audience. This process takes time, as she can search online the different clientele within her area. She would need to visit businesses within proximity and even shop the competitor. She will have to call other managers in the area on how they are approaching their market, etc. If you gave her this task and ask to have it completed within three hours, you might as well shoot yourself in the foot and hoping you won't bleed to death.

This is a great sales marketing strategy but, it comes with time and continued follow up. The sales manager can find herself defeated if the local businesses do not want to work with her or her services; possibly due to budgets or seasonal restrictions. She gets rejected by several "no's" until she finds a company willing to work with her. If she were to be left alone on this task without adequate follow up on a timely manner, the task would fail and she would be hesitant to pursue other things that would energize her; and keep her focused.

Team building is geared with this same approach. Showcased on the previous example, when you consistently follow up with her efforts, you are portraying a sense of trust and empowerment; thus leading to support the company vision altogether. Same holds true with staff members. You cannot expect that your new heightened way of thinking, being exposed to something inspiring for a moment, can immediately change the wave of downturn, hostility or lack of excitement that has plagued the company for months. But, I promise it will get there.

To fully understand the value of patience comes to mind the saying, "How can you eat an elephant? One bite at a time." In TLC's *My Strange Additions*, features a man who has literally eaten an entire commercial plane, piece by piece. That was the only way he said he could stay full. The fact remains, no matter how bizarre the need is, or how immense the feat, it can still be accomplished; adhering towards patience and determination. It will also take a team effort.

I am a big fan of Anthony Melchiorri's *Hotel Impossible* hosted on the Travel Channel. Before we got to know each other on a personal level, I learned that he became the best at the hotel and hospitality industry from engaging teams. In 1997, Melchiorri was appointed as general manager for the Lucerne, a hotel on the Upper West Side of New York City. Under his direction, the Lucerne was selected as the New York Times Travel Guide's Best Service Hotel. It took seven years to achieve such high merits and in today's world, that can seem like eternity. But, if you were living that type of excitement and change that Melchiorri spear-headed; time stood still and each day was a gift.

Taking time in creating proper processes such as hiring, promotions, cold call scripts, marketing procedures, etc. gives you an impacting result, as most managers only dream of the ability and flexibility to enjoy their time away from the company. Balance is essential when becoming a leader and building a successful empire. You owe it to yourself, as well as your clients, team members and family, the separate, balanced efforts in your part.

Upon reading, *Oola – Find Balance in an Unbalanced World* by Dave Braun and Troy Amdahl, it portrays the Seven F's for living a more fulfilled life: **Faith, Family, Field, Finance, Friends, Fitness**, and **Fun.** You do not dedicate 80 percent on *Field* and split the remaining 20 percent on the other six. Each one plays an important factor in your life and balancing it takes commitment, patience and time.

There is value on learning what the best experts of your field have done before you and follow their dedication. There is value on not having to re-create the wheel but enhancing it; giving it better tires or a better frame.

When you take the time to also train; instead of rushing to try and get any shift covered, you are promoting more value within your business. I see these types of mistakes often – everywhere I go. You can go to a grocery store, movie theater, or department store and have the cashier look at you blankly trying to remember the code for your avocado, popcorn, or leather jacket; forgetting all attributes of personality and service. They were placed in the forefront hastily, without adequate or proper training. Do you want substitute, warm body or do you want a team player? Do you want an ally or an enemy? This employee already wanted the job and told all her friends how excited she was when hired, to only be thrown in front of the first angry customer, who had to wait in line for a supervisor, because she only had 15 hours of training time and double charged the laundry detergent.

If you are wanting change in your business now, learn to be still and have patience. Learn that processes and products will be enhanced when you invest in the people. Understand that time can be your best ally if used appropriately; and with proper follow through, provides realistic goals for individual achievement. You have time to do it correct this first go around. Don't lose the opportunity.

On the training seminars I host, regarding my organization – *The Leadership Achievement Association*, I focus on a key rule when it comes to leading a successful team: **Have Fewer Rules for People.** You have probably heard of national, best-selling author and leader Stephen Covey, with his award-winning book, *The 7 Habits of Highly Effective People*. In it he shares the story on how he, a great orator and leadership expert; was taught a valuable lesson.

Covey is a soft spoken, well-mannered man who was sitting in a subway one day. He noticed some children were acting up and rambunctious all in front of their disconnected, lackadaisical father. After witnessing the constant jumping of the children, with the complete disregard of the people around them; he went over to the father and asked, "Sir, do you think you can do something about these children?" With a bewildered look, the man looked up, snapped back to reality and nodded, "Oh yes, sorry. We just left the hospital and their mother just died. I guess they don't know how to handle it yet, and clearly, neither do I."

At that moment, Covey felt terrible and embarrassed. He explains how all his assumptions of thinking this was an absent-minded parent, with selfish regard to those around him, were proven false. With his first reaction of irritation, led to the instant connection of sympathy. He immediately learned to have less rules for people. When you do this, you will envelope an understanding that some people are at a different moment in their lives than you, and that's ok.

I have had managers confess this was their wave of thinking; exuding frustrations when some of their employees not grasping the training as quickly as *they* did, when they were in that line-level role, only a few months in, or at their age and so forth. Understand that not everyone cannot pick up the rhythm of high work ethic, as well as you do, or have. Different individuals host different perspectives of their own lives at different moments. Trust they will understand the tasks at hand. You can then increase your strength of influence by taking on that responsibility and role of mentoring and leading them to discovery, instead of giving up on them.

A true leader will understand that the best things in life are attained when *earned*; and all through dedication and delayed gratification.

Principle #9:
PEOPLE BELIEVE WHAT YOU BELIEVE

This principle is one of the most paramount and necessary of all principles to adhere by. Every successful business and leader makes sure that every, single day is used to create a center of influence towards improving the team. Whether through profits, ranking, solutions, systems, branding, etc. If you create an atmosphere of betrayal, defeat, uncertainty, disloyalty, or disbelief, that this wave of thinking will make you the "good-guy" when times are tough - you're far from the truth.

When you're starting a new company or revamping or reconstructing the company employee module, the one prime action is recruiting those valuable team members. But, if you're hiring anyone out the gate, every good employer understands that there is one costly detriment as a result: turn-over.

So, ask yourself this question:
Do people want to work for you?

When you are in a position of expanding the company; you must have an underlying belief that those key players are a valuable piece to this growth, not just a replacement in the roster of a department.

Even if you have started Jim Smith Marketing, LLC, doesn't mean you are your own monopoly and no one else can leave your company to work for a competitor, because your niche is billboard ads for small businesses.

Every single company, brand or service has a direct or indirect competitor. This has been proven through online social media. From the sticky note pad you write on (and possibly sell) to the special energy drink you shake in your water; you have someone else competing against you. Potential clients for Jim Smith Marketing may not want billboard ads because they use the power of Instagram; so frankly, you may not stand out as much as you think you do.

What does that mean for growth? The team members that can be assets to promote your growth *must believe what you believe.*

What does this look like?

It doesn't matter if you are a marketing company competing against another marketing company who has 20+ years running over you. What truly matters is your belief that you can offer better products that are exactly in line with your audience now. That you are consistent with your efforts and you lead your team accordingly.

Many times I go to networking functions; everyone telling me their two minute elevator speech on what they *do*. I don't get a sense of *why* they do it. So, unfortunately, they fall back in the invisible Rolodex inside my head under "Sales Something ... something." My response when they ask me the same thing, "I lead a team of individuals who create a lasting experience for newcomers visiting Texas." This tends to get them more intrigued, and find *value* in what I do and who's on board with me. I couldn't say I was just a general manager at a hotel. There's so much more.

This is the same when interviewing. When you shift your questions on trying to understand how your needs can align with their skills and how you can also **help their own growth professionally**, it creates a sense of *partnership*. Everyone wants to feel valuable and able to contribute to something. When you just ask questions like, "Name your best achievement" only places you for an answer that you *want to hear* - which then short-lives the relationship they have with you and your company, because they've already achieved their best - at a different employer.

Turn-over is one of the most costly out of the P&L's in any business, and I didn't allow it any longer. Yes, this is 99% controllable. I spare that 1% for emergency transfers due to family, spouse moving, etc. But the rest is from how you are managing and leading your organization. It goes back to our prime lesson through this all:

People don't quit jobs, they quit people.

When you are leading the company, do you represent value in your employees? Or is there an invisible barrier of *fear,* thinking you will lose them anyway? You don't have to mention it, but leaving the paper "NOW HIRING" sign all year long, is one indicator of showing your current, and potential employees how you view your staffing model.

Stop wasting money and time on turn-over, causing burn-out for the ones whom "stuck it out" with you and now, due to their *seniority,* are exhausted from the overhaul of training new-hire after new hire.

Create value by implementing systems of expectation. Each member has a true, 60-90 day training period. No, not seven days. Instill the reasons why you are in business and that you want them here to help generate that vision further. Survey, survey, survey! When you receive feedback from your staff, you are including them in the process. When employees are felt like they are being pushed away from details, or information - they feel cheated, or undervalued. Do you like having to start over with different staff members? Start communicating ... to everyone.

Then, finally exhibit **respect.** When there is a culture of respect generated from the top down, saying hi to the janitor and having those same conversations you do as if you are talking to a department manager, will gain a better outcome towards your payroll. People believe what you believe and will want to work where they feel they are a great part of something.

You can even try to take monopolies and see if they don't have a competitor, justifying that those valuable key players, such as employees and clients won't leave due to this. In 1888, Cecil Rhodes received financing from gold and diamond magnate Alfred Beit and founded De Beers. De Beers, which has grown to encompass every aspect of the diamond trade, has a well-documented and well-established history of engaging in monopolistic practices.

The primary complaint leveled against the company is its purchasing and stockpiling of rough diamonds in order to inflate prices by controlling the available supply. With its control over a majority of the diamond mines in South Africa, Namibia and Botswana, De Beers ships vast quantities of rough diamonds to a clearing house in

London where they are individually graded, cataloged, and sorted. This massive cache of reserved product was used by the company to enforce the idea that diamonds are *scarce*.

On July 13, 2004, De Beers pleaded guilty to engaging in price-fixing on industrial diamonds and by 2012, the company's market share had plummeted to less than 50 percent, a far cry from the 90 percent share it had celebrated in the 1980s. People left and invested, as well as those who applied for employment, to smaller companies; which held credible and favorable backgrounds.

Nowadays, it is easy to start a company in almost any industry, with the use of the internet, platforms and video/audio online space. In order to stand above the noise of marketing campaigns from your competition, you have to amplify the strength and branding the belief in everything that you do and who you are.

During my training seminars, I hone in on the understanding that your title does not define who you are. Your title is a summary of responsibilities you have mastered through your work experience. Yes, it provides merit and is a great indicator of progression and professional development; but credibility and character cannot be summed by title alone, if at all.

How can you explain if things you assume are going to end up a certain way – and don't? We think successful businesses are a makeup of tons of money invested into it, a team of highly experienced individuals, notoriety and publicity. If this were the case, how come the vast majority of us haven't heard of the name, Samuel Pierpont

Langley?

Samuel Pierpont Langley was an American physicist with a few inventions under his belt. His resume was vast, including being an assistant at Harvard College Observatory, professor at the US Naval Academy, and was a secretary at the Smithsonian. Back in the early 1900's, piloting an aircraft was the wave of popularity in its era. It was like our own dot com experiences today. Langley wanted to be the first to build the airplane to hoist a man over the air. He hired several engineers and was given a $50,000 grant to do so. The New York Times followed him everywhere.

In a small town named Dayton, Ohio, there were two brothers named Orville and Wilbur Wright. They were also inventors, but in an extremely smaller scale. But, they had an staggering and unwavering belief they could invent the man-powered flight. They took proceeds from their bicycle shop to buy different parts and piece them together. They would head out for about five trips a day, knowing on average that was how many times they would crash, and all before dinner. No one on the Wright brothers' team had a college education and there was no publicity on who they were. Their strong belief and passion to contribute this to the world, was powerful enough to manifest success. And, on December 17, 1903 the Wright brothers took flight for the very first time, and no one was there to witness this. We only heard about it a few days later.

Langley, who had the money, the fame and the credibility of the best engineers at its day, had the belief to be first. When he got word that the Wright brothers were successful in achieving this, he quit. Langley could've added on to its build and partner to revolutionize the model altogether, but his *why* was focused on the money and fame. Money should never be the reason a company forms and exists. If Langley focused on true innovation, instead of wanting to be first, he wouldn't have stopped at only two crashes, and quit.

The Wright brothers had their strong beliefs on why they were doing what they were doing, and it turn, set the precedent for the rest of their team to put in the extra hours, repeated efforts after failed attempts, and diligence needed until succession. They did not seek fame or fortune, and yet have been one of the most influential pioneers of innovation ever known.

People believe what you believe. No one else is going to belief in your business or the success of your business *before* you do. If you're trying to foster a strong relationship with key business partners, increase your client retention and have more people work with you, purchase your products and become repeat customers – they must believe why you are in business at all. We talk about titles and managing a team. But, not one of those hold true to its core, if it does not align with your *why* and the services you want to contribute to the world, to make other people's lives better.

Make sure each and every day is dedicated towards the enhancement of your brand, by better training, better problem solutions and also feedback. You are cementing the growth of your company and your roster of allies triples.

US VERSUS THEM

Now take a step back for a second. Where are you in your current position? Do you hold the ability to create change? Yes, the answer is always yes. Regardless of title, you have accept the responsibility and allow the opportunity to take pride in making your current job, business and company a mark in your city, town and state.

An example of *us versus them* is found during training. Let's say you have the responsibility of hiring the new recruits on staff. What happens if your supervisor doesn't give you an added bump on your wage or training bonus – then what do you do? Does the resentment start forming against the company; and thus your training efforts start to dwindle down to the bare minimum?

When you create a sense of angst against your own managers, brand or company, due to reasons of not feeling proper validation from your job, and then representing this towards the clients and customers; you must keep in mind it is all coming from your lips first. We, as consumers do not see this unjust treatment from your manager, it is *you* we see. Your character is who you are, not the nametag you wear. You are immediately showing that *you* get easily bothered by a sense of unfairness or lack of praise from your team. What is worse if you are in a position of management. You may think this dogma can easily influence others when in actually it creates defense mechanisms for those people around you.

When I was a front desk supervisor, this role had small pockets of responsibility, but mostly covering shifts that were called off by another employee, possibly due to an emergency or other reasons. I was told to train on how to be personable with people. How do you train someone to care? I was told to make sure our scores were up. Wait, aren't there other team members responsible for these things? This all came from a general manager who would show up to work late and often times leaving early. She didn't even implement these same goals within her own leadership, thus delegating it off onto me.

I felt stuck. I felt that my talents were sorely abused and only placed on a stand-by basis. I learned early on that anything and everything I do must align with my purpose – my service to others; having an exhilarating experience through me and the company. Starting over at another job was not an option. It's too exhausting to keep "job-hopping", as many employees and managers do so if things aren't going the way they want.

By this belief, I started to appreciate the resources around me, such as late nights with freedom to learn the property management systems, read over our loyalty programs and master our bonus structures. I become fully knowledgeable about all our brands within our hotel chain, as well as our competitors. When all these free opportunities became available; I took advantage quickly and led whoever was willing to listen.

A sign of a strong leader is showcasing an ability to properly cross-train employees and having them learn new skills to perform tasks within other departments. This portrays balance within the team and in hopes of each individual employee to value what the other team members contribute; as well as how the company operates as a whole.

There was a housekeeper that always passed by the

front desk and could see me smiling, laughing and genuinely content with each guest. She approached me and asked if I could train her as a front desk agent, so she can help out in case someone called in sick. What a team player! I didn't know I was the influence, but, stated she wanted a piece of the fun too! Soon she was learning check-ins and billing during the down time.

Our own manager, however, was leery about the training because there is an invisible rule within hotels to not have housekeepers mesh with front desk agents; that it posed a distraction. When the housekeeper mastered the system within only a few short months; she took the different skill sets learned, applied herself in her own department and was eventually promoted. She took initiative at first, just because she was curious. Her growth was due to feeling valued and part of something bigger. It wasn't even for extra pay. She wanted to contribute. Guests absolutely loved her.

We then won the JD Power and Associates award for best extended-stay customer service shortly after these changes; and I glistened with pride. I knew it took a team effort, but the dynamic and culture that stemmed from knowing we had worked at it together. We even knew the fame and glory all went back to the general manager who, had shown little to no appreciation for us staff; but that didn't deter us from perceiving what we had to do day to day; into becoming something more than just a routine and collecting a paycheck.

At the forefront of any company whether you answer the phone, you greet clients at the door or are an independent contractor representing a bigger company - you are the first, last and sometimes only connection, impression, outlet, source of information, etc. for that client.

A big concern in today's small business startups, are its lack of genuine customer service. Since more and more individuals are hidden through their technical devices; a typical client only expresses five words to create a sentence, so he can have his extra shot, triple whipped latte for the day. However, employees find themselves in the direct line with a customer's wrath, if something went wrong with his triple, mocha – whatever; then having to fight the temptation of reprimanding that client; how dare they get upset!

When did treating people in exchange for goods and services become so brash and hostile? Pay attention to these signs from employees with the lack of wanting to contribute proper customer service. The majority of complaints stem from not being heard, when vocalizing a problem.

If you do not learn to listen, how can you expect your own employees do follow suit, especially to your potential customers? A brand, a product, a service, and even virtual market all share one thing in common – the client. They can be an integral part of your success as a business owner or manager, if they believe what you believe. Your own employees can also become your biggest fans, when they believe what you believe.

The beauty lies when you are able to solve problems with your own services and products. That is should a prime reason your company exists. Then lead and operate accordingly.

Principle #10:
GRASS ISN'T GREENER ON THE OTHER SIDE
IT'S GREEN WHERE YOU WATER IT

As natural creatures of habit, when change arises we either fight or flight. Often times this is the same in any industry – if you're not happy, you quit. When a person tries to tie his or her own happiness in directly correlation with what they *do*; they're setting their hopes up for failure and resentment.

Successful leaders understand the value of team collaboration. When a team is united, there are no questions about any member, nor management team members' motives. You feel a sense of protection towards your company and everyone on board feels the same way.

There is a local Mercedes Benz dealership that recorded a commercial, listing every team member on property. At first, I thought this was a waste of commercial dollars because it displays the expectation that Sally Smith (name changed), who is mentioned, is to greet you when you arrive? That seems so farfetched. Little did I know, that each team member has worked for that dealership for over 10-15 years individually! So yes, Sally will greet you when you arrive. Talk about pride and commitment!

These are teams that take pride in their products, make sure everyone on board is on the same page and same vision as well. The leaders of these strong teams, prioritize their impressions and reputation from the top down. Employees at the Mercedes Benz dealership do not covet the manager titles; because they have found purpose on their current roles today, to foster success for the company as a whole. Their state of mind, quality of life and relationships with their families are enhanced in doing so.

Often times you see a team struggling because they have no direction on whose lead to follow. There is lack of assertiveness and leadership in the management team. This harbors animosity and resentment, generated quickly amongst employees; then towards its clients and the trail continues. Is this something your company can afford – a tainted reputation?

Let's take personal relationships, for a moment. It is fun when you start seeing or dating someone. Every message, every phone call, every date becomes anticipating and exciting. When you progress, months down the road you find yourself in stagnation. Then you will tend to find fault in each other and how it is not fair to do this or do that. Finally, when the daily grind just seems too much; you falter into temptation. You part ways before dating someone new, or quit altogether. What happened here?

Are you are in your current position trying to load yourself with excuses on how employees aren't *stepping up*; or your clients are impossible to work with, all while trying to be a leader? Relationships, even work relationships fail due to lack of communicating certain expectations. But, there is no time to make excuses and blame outside exposures towards your leadership, or lack. A strong leader passionately continues to find ways on revamping the culture for the team; just like within marriages that surpass decades, still holding strong. They don't try and jump ship thinking something is better out there for them. They work on issues as they are now, and creating positive outcomes. A strong leader becomes a mentor and similar to starting a relationship, will hold consistency and support from the moment of hire, through its up and downs of turmoil, and leading it back to succession.

It is a natural tendency to explore what is on the other side; and if you're currently unhappy in your job, seeking approval from another industry or market, teeter-tottering, can get quite exhausting. Switch course if you are absolutely, in your core – know that what you are doing today, is not positively affecting or promoting growth on the three key components in your life: health, family and faith.

Don't chase money. As I mentioned earlier. money is always the result. If you are not getting paid what you feel you deserve at this time; doesn't give you a reason to keep quitting, trying to find that adequate pay somewhere else. Even though I was making great money as a store manager, my day to day grind were discussions on collecting debt and lending out a loan to someone who already has high debt; just to buy his child a new PlayStation. It didn't make any sense to me, nor justifying how I can contribute to this type of service any longer.

I knew the money was helping me live a comfortable life, but my health started to deteriorate. I simply missed talking to people, connecting with them. After several months of feeling this disconnect, I went to my doctor who then diagnosed me as being severely dehydrated and slightly depressed.

I couldn't do it anymore, even to think I "needed" the pay. I quickly reminded myself of what was truly important to me and what I enjoyed most - hotels! I loved providing excellent service to tourists and representing my city in its glory. I took an extremely large pay cut to become a front office supervisor; but put my head down, met incredible influencers and stayed focused. A short six years later, I was managing and opening multi-million dollar hotel properties, surpassing the payroll I thought I was never going to have again; forcing me to stick to a job that nearly got me hospitalized. That one decision of not chasing money and rather living with purpose, ultimately landed the opportunities and experiences I am most grateful for today.

I know several individuals who continue to stay at a job because of fear. If a job tends to have a husband miss several dinners with his wife and children; he is forced to quit or forever face the guilt when coming home late. There is no balance. Or, he cannot "afford" to quit, in fear of not finding another stream of income, so he presses on a job he loathes.

In retrospect, communication should be a key component in fostering the work/home balance. My husband Jason, always communicates within a few hours before the end of the day, just to let me know if he will be running late or if a colleague is wanting to meet with him. He doesn't just show up after dishes have been put away with his apologies. He portrays respect towards his commitment into his home and towards his career. This balance also avoids unnecessary problems, that may lead to having him resign from something he enjoys.

There are those that are forced to change jobs

because it just seems extremely difficult. I have many independent contractor colleagues who start a commission-based only career. However, they find themselves quitting early because they did not commit to their own expectations on what the job demanded; in order to be successful. They failed to ask themselves those important questions: how much risk will this take against their family and livelihood? How much sacrifice is needed?

There was one lure to the idea of becoming independent contractors, and that was seeing other successful agents buying the latest Maserati, taking 10-day vacations and having flexibility to watch their kids' soccer games. They convince themselves of the lifestyle before understanding the gruel and sacrifice these agents also endured. Then if the going gets tough, justifying that the grass on another field – another industry altogether, will solve all their problems.

The one example were success is manifested through adversity, even creating his career later in life, is the story of Jack Jameson, with Farmers Insurance Group.

Jack Jameson dedicates his time to his family, church and business – all equally. He started without a single dollar in the bank, 38 years old, deciding to become an insurance agent in a town less than 30,000 people and having about 10 other, experienced insurance agents in the same area. His district manager did give him a free book of leads. He called it the White Pages. Jack did not let competition, or a belief that odds were against him, and got to work. For the past 11 consecutive years employed at Farmers, he earned every bonus, every championship, every elite award made possible by the company, back to back. If you get a chance to sit in on his seminars, he speaks with so much passion and conviction about what he does. You feel his belief on the importance of his message; portraying the precedent of life insurance. Jameson represented himself, as he was, not trying to figure out how other people became successful. He doesn't have time to get distracted; or allows excuses to creep into his mind if something sets him back.

Understand that today, you have the right tools, the right opportunities, the right moment to create the changes needed in your life and to reach the fulfillment you are seeking. Harness the true magnitude of what you have now, don't see it as any worse. Appreciate that you are able to read this book, gain insight of developing yourself professionally and personally, and excite yourself with the idea that a great life is in store for you. This comes from commitment against the odds; not having to continuously start over in your contribution efforts to the world.

I take immense satisfaction in knowing that any business can work its way back to life; because I have experienced and witnessed these transformations first hand. Taking on almost de-flagged, monished hotels to award winning properties in a few months, is an ideal dream to almost any hotelier struggling in today's competitive hospitality world. This holds true to most small businesses against its competitor. Start your belief that you are able to become a true leader now; the one that we need to fuel our businesses, brands and companies into succession.

Become a center of influence and nurture a positive perspective, consistent follow-through and create a strong mantra of exceptional service with quality products. By now, you have a better understanding of your value and what you can contribute to the rest of us. When you tap into your purpose, especially when it comes to work; you unleash a greater understand of the word around you. And guess what, you have completed this book. I knew you could it. Take the momentum and pride of knowing you stayed focused, your committed yourself to these tools and now, it is up to you to implement and foster positive changes.

I am proud of you. I am your biggest fan and I'm excited for your journey.

ABOUT THE AUTHOR

A high performance expert – Pia Harriman is known for her ability to enhance the reputation of a company by building teams built on integrity, determination and service. She brings 14+ years in business as the "High-Performance Leader" by acquiring and managing multi-million dollar hotel properties at bottom ranks, turning it over to award winning brands within the nation.

What makes her feat different from professionals of this caliber, is her quick resolve and speedy turn-around, which results in higher profits, recognition and client and staff retention. Pia Harriman believes that the success for each individual company stems on the dedication brought forth regarding extraordinary team collaboration.

Placed on the fast track early on, Harriman began her exposure to business and high performance being the only female car salesperson at age 18. Her "training" manager forced her to close deals by promising *free* oil changes and *lifetime* car washes for those unsure of buying. She questioned this so, in turn his response was if this wasn't done nor stated, she will surely fail and be terminated within the first two weeks.

Car sales is a competitive market and not being exposed to the obscure stereotype of a "car sales agent"; it did not waiver why she applied in the dealership initially. She wanted to create an exhilarating experience to her clients from her service and products.

So Harriman go to work.

She learned the safety, luxury and performance features for all vehicles. She understood the different vehicles in specific tiers, as well as each horsepower and turbo engine that went to which specific model. By not adhering to the un-written "law" of broken promises, she kept to her integrity and grit, soon becoming the lead sales agent in the *entire* dealership, yielding over $1.3 million in sales – within her first 3 months employed.

Her general manager quickly offered the opportunity to earn over six-figures within the next several months, but in return, quitting school and dedicate all her efforts to the dealership. She could not understand the importance of the gruel in sacrifice to her education, so her formal resignation led to a new found passion – the hotel / hospitality industry.

Harriman took a gruesome pay-cut entering the hotel industry as a front desk agent. However, she felt she had much more to accomplish, than trying to work for adequate pay. Never been exposed to the industry, she succeeded to promote herself within her 90 day probation period to supervisor. Shortly, within a span of only eight years, Harriman quickly rose up in ranks to become the general manager – which led to leading and opening multi-million dollar hotel properties. Her company promoted her as their manager developer, to instill the same high performance strategies she's accomplished in turn, to train the rest of the company in succession. Some individuals of the same caliber take 20-30 years to merit this similar feat.

In March, 2014 Harriman acquired a new hotel property and earned $75,000 in sales from *one-single* client. The owner was quite shocked and jokingly announced, "Ok make us money ... but not too much!" This was achieved within the first month of acquisition, as well as other profits from the day to day sales she oversaw.

In July, 2014 she soon realized her efforts were bound for a larger audience, a grander scale. She broke off the hotel industry completely and became a licensed financial and insurance advisor for the state of Texas, where she could work one on one with individuals, protecting their most valuable assets.

In September 2014, only two short months in the Reserve Program with Farmers Insurance Group, she was appointed as an exclusive agency owner. This probationary period stems from 120 days and on-going. She completed the program in 55 days; top 9 percent of the entire district.

In January 2015, she launched the ***Leadership Mastery Academy*** which focuses on entrepreneurial development, branding and recognition. These are a package of online and LIVE workshop events, phone conferencing and training, audio programs, as well as personal one on one coaching geared to be completed within a few short weeks; in similarity to the quick time-frame of her own achievements.

Harriman is also known for her fervor towards connecting people; in turn webbing a network of like - minded professionals, geared in relationship to aiding each other's better practices, regarding business and social economics. Her elusive and persevering character has pioneered the wave of inspirational leadership; a catalyst to ongoing training measures for the next generation of management and principals. In turn, forming her organization, ***The Leadership Achievement Association*** which connects individuals from all over the nation to exchange ideas and personal success stories and professional development strategies.

Harriman is also the author of "**The Highest Paid Employee – 10 Principles of Leadership**". The book reveals strategies to regain focus on enhancing professional and personal relationships, strengthen a positive and result-oriented influence, as well as living a more fulfilled life - all starting with your own contribution at the workplace.

In April, 2015 she successful launched The Highest Paid Employee Podcast Series on iTunes. Here she discusses the same values and strategies found in the book; as well as interviews from leaders and influencers all over the world.

Harriman is a wife, mother, entrepreneur, author, VIP and keynote speaker and philanthropist. Her passion, loyalty and dedication coinciding with each mission statement, company morale and group or individual goals; whether personal or professional, has been her lifeblood and continues.

Some of the best leaders came from being employees, who looked at how you managed - and knew they had to be **different.**

-Pia Harriman

www.ingramcontent.com/pod-product-compliance
Lightning Source LLC
Chambersburg PA
CBHW030802180526
45163CB00003B/1132